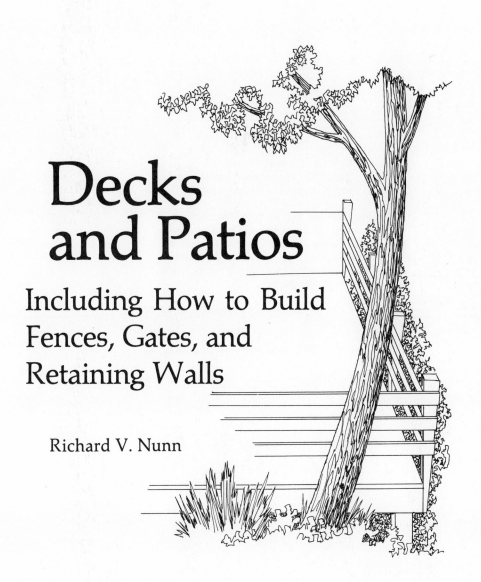

Decks and Patios

Including How to Build Fences, Gates, and Retaining Walls

Richard V. Nunn

OXMOOR HOUSE, INC.
Birmingham, Alabama

Library of Congress Catalog Card Number: 76-40860
ISBN: 0-8487-0452-5

Manufactured in the United States of America

First Printing 1977

Decks and Patios

Editor: Candace Conard-Franklin
Cover Photograph: Joe Benton
Photography: Andy Hartley, Bob Lancaster, California
            Redwood Association, Simpson Timber Co.,
            Portland Cement Co.

Contents

INTRODUCTION. 4
  Financing. 4
  Remodeling Contractors 5

MATERIALS. 6
  Dimension Lumber and Boards 6
  Plywood. 7
  Moldings 8
  Hardboard 8
  Railroad Ties 8
  Sand and Gravel. 8
  Brick and Stone 17
  Concrete. 17
  Basic Fasteners. 17
    Nails. 17
    Screws 18
    Specialty fasteners 18

DECKS 19
  Deck Building Techniques. 19
  Material Considerations. 20
  Post and Joist Support
    Techniques. 22
  Basic Plan for Deck Building 23
  Deck Finishes. 30
  Special Features for Decks. 30
  Deck Ideas. 36

FENCES AND GATES. 39
  Fence and Gate Materials. 40
  Fence Design and Dimensions. . . . 40
  Post Setting Details 46

Wooden Gate Details. 51
Joining Techniques 52
Installing Chain Link Fencing. . . . 56
Fencing Ideas. 59

PATIOS. 61
  Patio Design Considerations 61
  Concrete Patios 61
    Preparing the ground 62
    Building concrete forms. 62
    Placing the concrete. 66
    Finishing the concrete 70
    Curing the concrete. 71
    Building a bull float. 72
    Mixing your own concrete. 73
  Bricks-on-Sand Patios 75
    All about bricks. 75
    Grading and preparing the forms. . . 76
    Laying the bricks 76
  Flagstone Patios 79
    Laying the flagstone 79
  Wooden Patios. 82
  Patio Ideas 84

RETAINING WALLS. 85
  Concrete Block Retaining Walls. . . 86
  Brick Retaining Walls 88
  Concrete Retaining Walls 91
  Railroad Tie Retaining Walls. 92
  Stone Retaining Walls 93

INDEX. 95

Introduction

You will have a lot of fun with this book.

In addition, you will gain a great deal of personal satisfaction and a feeling of accomplishment.

All of the decks, patios, fences, gates, and retaining walls presented here are easy to do. None of the projects is very complicated in design or building technique, and your new deck, patio, fence, or whatever will add to the value of your home as well as to your own pleasure.

Most of the projects presented here may be completed in a relatively short amount of time. Therefore, you do not have the "weekend handyman hangover" that takes three or four additional weekends from which to recover. There is little "finish" involved in building decks, patios, and fences. You will find this lack of detail a relief from other how-to projects.

Decks and Patios includes ideas for designing your own projects as well as instructions on how to build these structures. The how-to instructions are basic; that is, steps needed to complete a specific project are not given, simply because projects will vary from reader to reader. But you can be sure that whatever the project, the techniques to accomplish it are included in this book. You have only to adapt the basic techniques to fit your particular project and design.

The effort you expend in building an outdoor structure will be an investment in your home and future that you and your friends will enjoy for years. But even more important will be your satisfaction in doing the job yourself.

Financing

A small deck, patio, fence, or retaining wall should not be exorbitantly expensive, but you may need a small home improvement loan to get the job done all at once. There are several alternative methods for financing a building project.

Short-term and revolving credit. If your project is not going to cost too much (about $600), the building retailer or home center where you buy materials will often extend you credit. The revolving credit plan extends the payment period for 30 days (but sometimes 28 days), interest free.

If you must take more than 30 days to pay for the materials, you will usually be charged interest on the balance. Be sure to check out the interest rates which retailers are required by law to tell you. The interest percentage is usually 1½ percent per month, or 18 percent per year.

Some retailers are now offering a ceiling charge account. With this type of account, you may charge from $300 to $500 and pay it back on an installment plan. Again, the interest is usually 18 percent per year, but be sure to check it out before you sign any agreement.

Bank loans. You may be able to borrow money for your project from a bank on your signature if a lot of money is not involved. Do not consolidate any other loans you may have with a home improvement loan. Should you hire a contractor to do the job and the contractor arranges the financing for you, *do not* permit the contract to place a lien on your property.

Conventional home improvement loans. Many savings and loan associations, banks, mutual savings banks, and commercial banks will lend money on home improvements. This type of loan, however, varies according to the availability of money the lenders have to lend. You can usually gauge the availability of money by advertisements run by financial companies in your local newspaper and on local television and radio.

Credit unions. If you belong to a credit union, be sure to ask the director for information about a home improvement loan. Usually, the interest rates are well within reason, and there is plenty of time to repay the loan.

Finance companies. Finance companies are usually the last resort for a home improvement loan. There is nothing wrong with accredited finance companies; it is just that interest rates can be very high, and the repayment arrangements may be difficult to comply with. Have the company answer all your questions satisfactorily before you sign such a loan agreement.

Open-end mortgages. If your project will be a large one financially, and you have not yet paid off the mortgage on your home, you may have an open-end clause in the mortgage that allows you to borrow money equal to the mortgage principal you have already paid. In fact, the interest rate on the money may be the same interest you are paying now on the mortgage.

Reworking existing mortgages. Cash for home improvements is sometimes made available by simply refinancing your present mortgage. This is a good possibility if the cost of your deck or patio or fence project is large. However, the cost of money today may prohibit this move, especially if you have a low interest rate on your present mortgage. It is worth checking into, especially if the improvement loan will be for a large sum of money.

Remodeling Contractors

If you decide that you do not want to build that fence or patio yourself and want a contractor to do it for you, there are several guidelines you should follow:

- Get at least three different bids on the project.
- Check out each bidding contractor with the local Chamber of Commerce or Better Business Bureau.
- Do not let a contractor finance the job with a lien on your home as part of the financial arrangement.
- Have the contractor give you a written contract including an estimate on the work to be done. Insist on this.
- Make sure the cost of the work to be done is the *total* cost.
- Make sure the contractor obtains the proper building permits.
- Have the contractor give you a schedule of the work to be done: the starting date and the finishing date. Hold the contractor to this schedule, unless circumstances occur over which the contractor has no control.
- Do not give the contractor money in advance for work to be completed. The contractor may request installment payments as certain stages of the work are completed. This is an acceptable procedure if the work to that point has been satisfactory. The usual arrangement is one-third of the fee when the job is half done, another third on completion, and the balance of the fee when all necessary certificates are obtained from the contractor.
- Have a firm arrangement with the contractor on how payment is to be made, particularly if subcontractors are involved in the project.
- Do not sign any agreement with a contractor until you have thought over the job and your financial obligation for at least three days.

Materials

Decks, patios, retaining walls, walks, fences, and other garden structures all involve materials that are usually available at either building materials retailers, home center stores, ready-mixed concrete dealers, or gravel and stone dealers. For prefabricated fences, do not overlook general merchandise stores, as well as the retailers listed above.

Since decks, patios, retaining walls, etc. are built from such basic materials as plywood, hardboard, lumber, boards, concrete, and brick, you should become familiar with what is available and know how to buy these materials. Each chapter also discusses the materials needed for particular projects in greater detail.

Dimension Lumber and Boards

There are two classifications of dimension lumber and boards: softwood and hardwood. Softwoods, such as hemlock, fir, pine, cedar, cypress, and redwood, may be used for framing. Hardwoods, such as oak, maple, birch, mahogany, and walnut, are acceptable to use for framing and finish work, but these materials are expensive and may be prohibitive for most outdoor structures. Softwoods other than cedar, redwood, or cypress should be chemically treated to prevent rot. You can buy a rot-preventive chemical at most building materials retailers. Follow the manufacturer's recommendations on the label of the container.

Dimension lumber is lumber that is 2 inches thick in nominal size (as it comes from the sawmill). When you purchase 2 by 4s, 2 by 6s, and 2 by 8s, you are buying *dimension* lumber.

Boards are 1 inch thick in nominal size. For example, 1 by 2s, 1 by 4s, and 1 by 6s are boards. Although you order and buy the lumber and boards according to their nominal size, the actual size—after shrinking and planing—is what you take home. (See chart Basic Lumber and Board Sizes.)

Boards and lumber are specially graded according to basic classifications: *common lumber*, which has defects and is used for construction and general-purpose building projects; and *select lumber*, which is sound and of good quality and is used when appearance is important.

The best grade of common lumber is No. 1, which contains only a few tight knots and blemishes and is suitable for stain or paint, or may be left "natural." No. 2 has larger knots and blemishes and can also be painted or stained; No. 3 has loose knots and flaws and should be used where the wood will not show; No. 4 also has many knots, is considered an economy grade, and should be used only where the wood will not show.

The grades of select lumber are B and Better (or 1 and 2 clear), which has only tiny imperfections; C select grade, which has limited imperfections; and D select grade which has many imperfections and is sometimes covered with a coat of paint to hide the defects.

Lumber and boards are sold by the board foot. A board foot is 1 inch thick, 12 inches wide, and 12 inches long. Building materials retailers will compute

Basic Lumber and Board Sizes		
Lumber type	Nominal size (inches)	Actual size (inches) (Material surfaced four sides and kiln dried.)
Boards	1x2	¾x1½
	1x3	¾x2½
	1x4	¾x3½
	1x5	¾x4½
Boards	1x6	¾x5½
	1x7	¾x6½
	1x8	¾x7½
Dimension	2x4	1½x3½
	2x6	1½x5½
	2x8	1½x7¼
	2x10	1½x9¼

the measurements for you; you need compute only the linear foot and width dimensions.

An excellent hint when buying lumber is not to overlook good used lumber. The chances are that the prices will be lower than new lumber, and used lumber is often better material than the new. It may look dirty, but this lumber is dried out, generally straight, and easy to work with.

Plywood

Plywood sheets are available in two faces: hardwood-faced and softwood-faced. Most outdoor structures call for softwood-faced plywood. Generally, the faces of this material are fir, but pine and spruce are sometimes used.

Most plywood is subject to industry grading standards which assure you that the material purchased is uniform. There are standards that permit plugging knotholes and mending split voids. This does not mean, however, that the material is of inferior quality; grading standards simply assure that you get what you pay for. Most plywood is graded by the American Plywood Association

(APA) and bears a backstamp or edge mark on the panel. This mark is your assurance that the plywood has been manufactured to the quality standards and performance requirements of the Association.

The following grading information is designed to give you some working knowledge when talking to a plywood dealer. With the dealer's help, select the plywood best suited to your project and your budget.

Softwood-faced plywood is manufactured in exterior and interior types. You will be working with exterior type plywood for outdoor structures discussed in this book. Exterior grade plywood is water resistant and is suited to permanent outdoor applications and to those projects that are subject to constantly moist conditions or extremely high humidity.

Veneer grades are designated according to the appearance quality of the face and back veneer and are indicated by the following letters:

N-grade is a special order, "natural finish" veneer. It may be all heartwood or all sapwood and is free of open defects. This grade does allow some repairs. N-grade is in limited supply and is very expensive. You probably will not use this material for any outdoor project except for a special garden structure that has to be smartly constructed.

A-grade is smooth and paintable; neatly made repairs are permissible.

B-grade is a solid surface veneer. Circular and other non-tapered repair plugs and tight knots are permitted.

C-grade permits limited splits and minimum veneer on some exterior-type plywood.

C-plugged is improved C-grade veneer with splits limited to ⅛ inch in width and with knotholes and borer holes limited to ¼ inch by ½ inch.

D-grade permits knots and knotholes to 2½ inches in width and ½ inch larger under certain specified limits; limited splits are permitted.

Where the plywood will show, consider A- or B-grade veneers. When appearance is not important, use C-grade, C-plugged, or D-grade faces.

Softwood-faced plywood is designated by group to indicate its stiffness and strength and the species of wood it contains. The groups range from 1 through 5 with the stiffest and strongest woods in Group 1.

You can purchase veneer grade combinations. For example, when the face will show and the backing will not show, choose an A-grade front and C-grade back. Generally, the glue bonds are classified as waterproof, water resistant, and dry.

Thicknesses of softwood-faced plywood are ¼, ⅜, ½, ⅝, ¾, and 1 inch.

Moldings

Molding patterns are so varied that a list here would be impossible. The ones you will be interested in for outdoor structures include quarter round, parting strip, and screen moldings.

Moldings are sold by the linear foot; the configuration or shape of the molding determines the price.

Hardboard

Hardboard panels are really wood. The material is made from wood chips that are turned into sheets under heat and pressure. There are two types of hardboard: standard and tempered. Tempered hardboard is preferred for outdoor use; it has been specially treated to withstand moisture.

Sizes of hardboard panels range from 4 by 4 to 4 by 16 feet, with the standards set at 4 by 8 and 4 by 10 feet; thicknesses are ⅛, ³/₁₆, ¼, and ⁵/₁₆ inch.

Hardboard manufacturers also have special trim moldings available. These include snap-on metal moldings for vertical joints, inside and outside corners, and cap moldings. Or you can use regular wood moldings such as batten strips, covers, and others.

Railroad Ties

Once upon a time you could pick up used railroad ties for free, but times have changed.

Railroad ties are still available, but they are difficult to locate. Ties are sold by the unit; one tie constitutes one unit. Your best sources are a railroad company, building materials retailer, garden supply center, home center store, and, of all places, antique shops.

Sand and Gravel

Sand and gravel are usually sold by the cubic yard. However, you may purchase them by the pound, depending on the dealer. Generally, a building materials retailer or home center store will sell sand and gravel by the bag with so many pounds to the bag. Concrete dealers sell the material by the cubic yard.

Sand, gravel, and crushed stone are referred to as *aggregates* when they apply to the composition of concrete. This material makes up 60 to 75 percent of the finished concrete mixture; the strength of the concrete is influenced by

(Continued)

Large paving bricks make up this handsome patio. The used bricks were laid on a concrete base and the joints filled with concrete. The effect is one of a worn cobblestone street and blends in beautifully with the house and the garden.

This brick-on-sand patio is laid in the popular herringbone pattern. The joints between the bricks are dusted with sand every year to deter plant growth. The patio acts as the perfect transition from house to garden.

Rough-sawn redwood boards nailed tightly together create a perfect garden backdrop, add architectural interest to an adjoining ranch-style home, and provide privacy. Plastic insets were used along each support post; the interesting post caps were sawn from 6 by 6s. A detailed diagram of this redwood and plastic fence appears in the chapter on Fences and Gates.

This board and board fence screens a yard from the street traffic. The fence appears the same from both sides and is designed to permit air to circulate freely. The fencing material is unfinished redwood; in time, weathering will turn the wood to a beautiful silver tone. The fence is slightly curved along its length to conform to the concrete curbing. For a detailed diagram of board and board fence building techniques, see the chapter on Fences and Gates.

This multilevel deck is enhanced by open screening and by a wide board fence that may act as a backdrop for plantings. The deck is located on a small lot and takes advantage of the sloping ground. The wide, boxed-in benches along the fence give the feeling of another deck level.

Facing page:

This deck provides a nice transition from the family room to a brick-on-sand patio. The L-shaped benches provide a perfect conversation area. Plants help spark this deck/patio combination, and the natural color clay pots blend with the colors of the brick and wood materials.

A low-profile redwood deck/patio is a natural extension of the glass-enclosed living area of this interesting home. The benches provide extra seating space in addition to giving the outdoor living area an enclosed feeling. Note how the dimensions of the decking, benches, and vertical support materials blend with the architecture of the house and with the natural landscaping.

Overleaf:

Tiles laid on sand and outlined with closely manicured grass create an interesting garden patio. Because of the moisture in the garden area, the tiles have taken on an attractive, mossy patina. The square pattern of the tiles blends perfectly with the gothic arches of the house and the small decorative fountain.

A cliff lot dictated the need for two decks here. One deck may serve as an entranceway into the house. The lower deck offers a spectacular view and is used primarily for entertaining. Steps from the lower deck may lead to the water. Both deck levels were built around trees to preserve the natural beauty of the landscape. Diagrams and instructions for building decks around trees appear in the Decks chapter under Special Features for Decks.

the correct ratio of fine to coarse aggregate.

Fine aggregate is usually sand that will go through a ¼-inch screen wire. It should be clean as well as free of any foreign substances.

Coarse aggregate may be either gravel or crushed stone; the size will range from ¼ to 1½ inches; it should be clean and hard and free of any organic or vegetable substances.

Brick and Stone

Bricks are sold by the unit; one brick constitutes one unit. Stone is sold either by the piece or by the square yard, depending on the dealer. Some slate is sold by the square yard, and you must lay out the slate to make up this measurement.

Stone is often graded into types and you pay for this refinement. For example, *dressed stone* is stone that has been chipped and chiseled into a finished shape; it is expensive. *Undressed stone* is inexpensive; no work has been done on it. *Semidressed stone* has been chiseled and chipped to approximate size so that you have a uniform selection. You also can buy *artificial stone* which is usually cheaper than dressed or semidressed stone. Artifical stone is referred to as cast stone, precast stone, imitation stone, and reconstructed stone.

Concrete

Ready-mixed concrete is sold by the cubic yard. There are 27 cubic feet in a cubic yard. If your project is an extensive one, it is much easier to purchase ready-mixed concrete instead of renting a cement mixer and stirring up your own batch. Most ready-mixed concrete companies insist on a minimum order of 4 cubic yards. To order the concrete, give the dealer the dimensions of the walk, driveway, patio, or whatever you are working on. This measurement should include width, length, and depth.

Cement is a dry powder that hardens when it is mixed with water and allowed to "set" for a period of time. Cement is the hardening ingredient in dry-mix products which are available in bags, to be mixed with water for final use. There are three types of dry-mix cement products:

1. Concrete mix. This material is designed for strength. The strength exceeds 4000 pounds per square inch. Use this type for walkways and porch foundations, when a relatively large volume is needed.
2. Sand mix. The designed strength exceeds 5000 pounds per square inch. Use this material for setting field stone, grouting, patching cracks, and topping.
3. Mortar mix. The designed strength exceeds 1250 pounds per square inch. Use it for laying brick, stone, and concrete block.

Basic Fasteners

To build fences, gates, patios, and other outdoor structures, you will need nails, screws, reinforcing wire and rod, and joist hangers. Separate listings for hardware requirements are given in the respective chapters. General nail and screw sizes and masonry anchor information are included here.

Nails

Nails are specified by inches and "penny" sizes. The penny size (which also refers to length) is noted by the letter *d*. A 5-penny nail, for example, is specified as 5d on the package and is 1¾ inches long. The diameter (gauge) of the nail almost always increases with the length of the nail.

The nail size you use is determined by the thickness of the wood you are nailing. The nail should be about three times longer than the thickness of the wood so that when you drive a nail, two-thirds of the nail will be in the wood and one-third will be in the material attached to the wood. For best results, always try to fasten a thinner piece of material to a thicker piece. Nails hold best in wood when they are driven at a slight angle.

Specialty nails include concrete nails, made with round, square, and fluted shanks; aluminum, copper, brass, stainless steel, bronze, and Monel metal nails.

Galvanized steel nails or aluminum nails are best for most exterior jobs since these nails will not rust. Aluminum nails are more expensive than galvanized nails, but they are more resistant to rust.

Screws

Screws are numbered according to length and gauge (diameter). Lengths of the screws range from about ¼ inch to 6 inches, in various gauges.

When you use screws, adopt the same length formula as that for nailing: one-third of the screw length should go through the top piece of material; two-thirds of the length should go into the base material.

Screw types include oval head, flathead, roundhead, and Phillips. Flathead screws are countersunk (recessed) flush with or below the surface of the material. For these screws you will need a countersinking bit—a tool to recess holes for flathead screws—attached to a brace to make this taper in the wood. If you have a portable electric drill, special countersinking attachments are available for use with it.

Oval head and roundhead screws are not countersunk. Phillips screws may or may not be countersunk, depending on the head type. You can purchase washers for screws; the washers provide a greater bearing surface for screw heads and also have a decorative feature.

Specialty fasteners

You may need special fasteners if you plan to fasten framing to a concrete surface. In such cases, the choice of fasteners includes anchors, lag screws, and concrete nails. If you decide to use anchors, you must first drill a hole in the concrete; then tap the anchor into the hole with a hammer. The lag screw is slipped through the material you want to fasten and twisted into the masonry anchor. The anchor will expand in the hole in the concrete and grip the sides of the hole.

Lag screws may be used without masonry anchors to hold wooden and metal ledger strips to the side of a house or structure such as a gate. Lag screws are sold per unit and are available in a range of diameters (gauge) and lengths.

Glue is another fastener that may be called for in building your project. For outdoor use, two adhesives are recommended: aliphatic resin and casein or latex glues. Aliphatic resin has a very fast drying time and is water resistant. Casein or latex glue dries slower than aliphatic glue, but it resists heat and water well, and the glue dries clear.

Decks

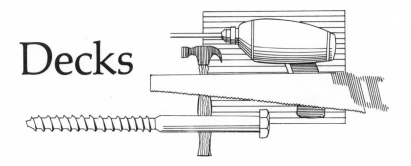

Many homeowners find themslves faced with the question of whether they should build a deck or a patio.

This chapter will help guide you in making your decision. There are so many variables involved, and project needs so differ with each reader, that a "thinking checklist" will aid you in making the final decision.

As a frame of reference, a *deck* is a raised wooden structure. A *patio* can be concrete, brick, flagstone, or concrete block. An entire chapter is devoted to patios later in this book; turn to that chapter after reading this one to help you with your decision.

Decks and patios are equally easy to build. A deck, for the most part, should blend in with the architectural design and appointments of your home. A patio also should blend in with architecture, but because it is usually placed on grade level, it should blend more with the landscaping.

A deck generally costs more to build than a patio. But an average-size job—nothing fancy or unique in structure, such as a deck on a hillside or in a gully or perched on a mountain cliff—should be within most homeowners' budgets.

A deck is generally constructed in sections: the framing, the decking, and the rails. A patio, if it is concrete, has to be done at once. However, if the patio is brick or flagstone, it may be constructed in stages.

As to skill, it takes more knowledge of materials to build a deck than a patio. A deck requires some basic wood-working skills; a patio requires fast action and a little knowledge about working with concrete.

Decks are ideal additions to homes with sloping lots because decks can be easily leveled to suit a sloping terrain. A deck is really a big floor, and this floor can be adjusted to fit the walk-out level of your living room or family room or bedroom. Or the deck may be constructed in several levels, each connected by a step or two. Decks, therefore, are more adaptable to the house and its lot than are patios. This could be a big consideration in your selection between the two.

The size of a deck—or patio—should be at least 8 by 10 feet. Of course, this may not always be possible. The best gauge is to build a deck or patio as large as your space and your budget can handle. You will be amazed at how fast the space will fill—with planters, outdoor furniture, and friends.

Deck Building Techniques

As mentioned earlier, a deck is nothing more than a floor. Whether it is constructed in one level or in multiple levels, the framing remains about the same as for a floor. Think in "floor" terms when you get into construction methods. These terms are as follows:

- Base support
- Ledger strips to hang joists onto the side of your home

- Joists spaced 16 or 24 inches on center
- The decking—or "floor boards"— which spans the joists
- Railings and steps

Since a deck is a true structure, consult the local building codes and ordinances before you begin ordering deck materials. And if you are in doubt about your property lines, check this out, too. You do not want to build a deck closer to a neighbor's lot than regulations permit.

To build a deck, follow these basic procedures:

- Think about what your needs are now and what they will be in the future. This should give you a rule of thumb to follow on the size and style of the deck.
- Examine the deck ideas in this book. Then look over deck ideas in monthly and annual magazines found on any newsstand. In addition, do not overlook literature on decks that is usually available at building materials retailers, home center stores, general merchandise stores, and special plan services. The special plan services advertise in monthly magazines; the cost of plans—or specifications—are nominal.
- Sketch out the plan you decide on, using graph paper. Include your house, the property lines, all trees, and other plants, underground service lines, walks, and so forth. Do not leave anything out. Next sketch in the proposed deck; see how it will fit in with all the other elements—the best angle, height, and styling.
- Check your local building codes; this is a *must*.
- Tell your neighbors about your building plans.
- If you do not want to build the deck yourself, consult a good, honest builder in your community. Get at least three bids before you sign any agreements. And, after you make a contractor choice, consider your decision for at least three days before you sign any agreement.

- If you choose to build the deck yourself, take the sketch to your local building materials retailer or home center. Discuss your project with these retailers. They may be able to save you money.
- Order the materials.
- Plan the job in stages: 1) the foundation work, 2) the framing, and 3) the finishing.

Material Considerations

You will find most of the basics on materials in the Materials chapter in this book. However, when you build a deck, a few additional points on choosing materials should be stressed.

Use redwood, cedar, or cypress for the deck. This material is rot and insect resistant. The material will cost more than treated lumber and boards, but it is worth the added expense for you not to be faced with a rotting deck within a few years.

If the deck will have to support a lot of weight, such as bench seats, planters, and so forth, on the deck floor—buy lumber than has no knots or only small knots. If the lumber has large knots, these knots should be positioned over joists or other substructure supports. You may have to lay the decking over the joists and shuffle the various pieces in order to properly position the knot. It is worth the time.

This section includes four charts. The Unseasoned Boards, Strips, and Dimension Lumber chart gives the nominal standard selling sizes and surfaced (dressed by a planer) sizes for garden grades of redwood. The span allowance tables are based on non-stress-graded redwood used in a single span. If you are going to load the deck with planter boxes, however, purchase shorter spans of lumber or larger beams and joists. Your building materials retailer will help you calculate this; the information here is to give you an idea of what will be required in framing and decking.

UNSEASONED BOARDS, STRIPS, AND DIMENSION LUMBER

Thickness								
Nominal	¾	1	1¼	1½	2	3	4	6
Surfaced on one or two sides	11/16	25/32	1 1/16	1 5/16	1⅝	2 9/16	3 9/16	5⅝

Width						
Nominal	3	4	6	8	10	12
Surfaced	2 9/16	3 9/16	5⅝	7½	9½	11½

SUGGESTED JOIST SPANS
For non-stress-graded redwood lumber with a live load of 40 pounds per square foot*

Joist Size		Construction Heart and Construction Common
2 x 6	16″ on center	6'–0″
	24″ on center	5'–0″
	36″ on center	4'–0″
2 x 8	16″ on center	9'–0″
	24″ on center	7'–6″
	36″ on center	6'–0″
2 x 10	16″ on center	13'–0″
	24″ on center	11'–0″
	36″ on center	9'–0″

*live load = an unconstant weight load—people

SUGGESTED BEAM SPANS
For non-stress-graded redwood lumber with a live load of 40 pounds per square foot and a dead load of 10 pounds per square foot

Beam Size	Grade	Width of Deck			
		6'	8'	10'	12'
4 x 6	Construction Grade Construction Heart Construction Common	Span 4'–6″	Span 4'–0″	Span 3'–6″	Span 3'–0″
4 x 8	Construction Heart Construction Common	6'–0″	5'–0″	4'–6″	4'–0″
4 x 10	Construction Heart Construction Common	7'–6″	6'–6″	6'–0″	5'–6″

SUGGESTED DECKING SPANS
For non-stress-graded redwood lumber with a live load of 40 pounds per square foot

Size	Grade	Span
2 x 4	Construction Grade Heart and Construction Grade Common	24″
2 x 6	Construction Grade Heart and Construction Grade Common	36″

Post and Joist Support Techniques

Post sizes should be 4 by 4 or 4 by 6 inches for *most* deck supports. Sink the supports at least 24 inches in the ground.

However, the depth of these footings depends on soil conditions, wind factors, and the depth of soil freezing in your area. Check with the local building department or ask your building materials retailer for advice.

The best way to support a post in the ground is with a concrete foundation. The first four drawings illustrate various concrete footings: A—concrete collar, B—nailing block, C—post anchor, and D—drift pin. Drawing E shows a simple technique; the earth is tamped around the support post. This final method does not provide adequate support for substantial decking projects and should be used only for small, low decks.

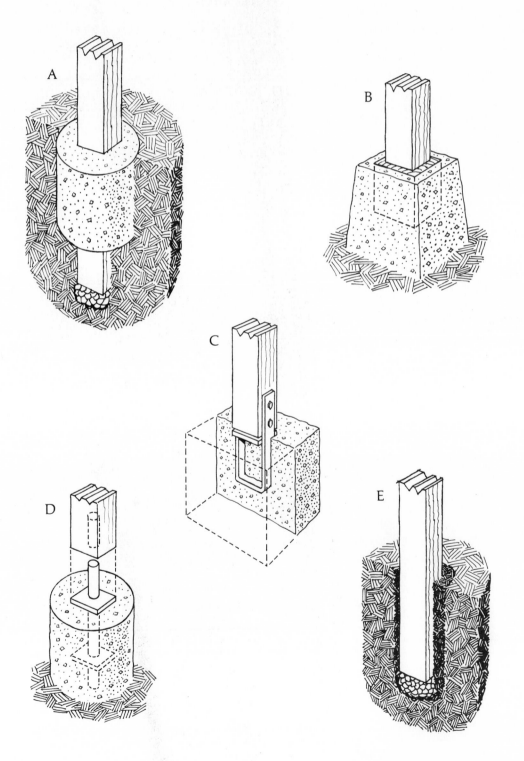

The footing and post anchor technique shown here is an excellent, substantial footing. It is easy to construct with ready-to-mix cement, but there is some margin for error in aligning the anchors. Regardless of their height, the posts must be perfectly plumb (vertically level).

Basic Plan for Deck Building

The deck in the following drawings was designed by Simpson Timber Co. It is a basic deck; from this design, with some modifications, you can build almost any deck.

The top part or floor of the deck is called the *decking.* The decking rests on *joists.* The joists are the primary structural element of the deck.

The joists sit on *beams.* The beams gather the weight load and transmit the weight to the *post* or *ledgers.* A ledger is nothing more than a board that is nailed or screwed to the face of an existing structure.

The posts rest on concrete *footings.* These footings, shown earlier, are in the ground and are generally placed concrete, although they may be concrete block.

The placement and height of a deck is your first consideration. The deck's position in relation to a doorway is important. Keep the deck as close to the floor level of your home as possible, or else try to position the deck so that you will have a very easy step down from the doorway. A good dimension to consider for deck floor heights is 1 inch below the doorway or from 4 to 7 inches below the doorway. After you establish this measurement, draw a *bench mark* or height mark on the side of the house. The entire deck will be built on the basis of this mark, so make sure it is horizontally level.

If your deck is to be a low deck—that is, if the decking will not be elevated high off the ground surface (grade level)—you may be able to place the joists directly on the footings without the use of support posts.

The deck illustrated in these drawings is less than 3 feet high. However, the deck, with longer support posts and bracing, could be built as high as 10 feet. The deck could also be built in multiple levels. Study the design here and see how the structure is constructed; once you know these basics, you can build most any deck.

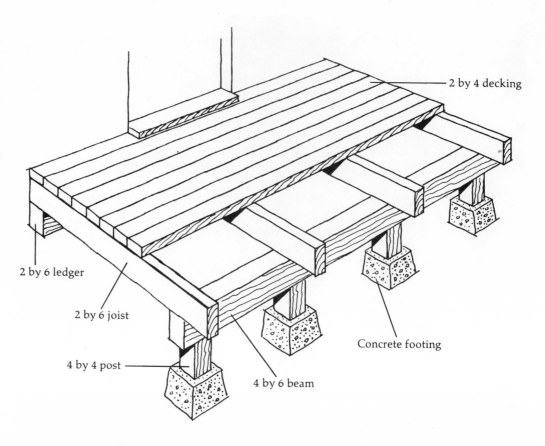

2 by 4 decking

2 by 6 ledger

2 by 6 joist

4 by 4 post

4 by 6 beam

Concrete footing

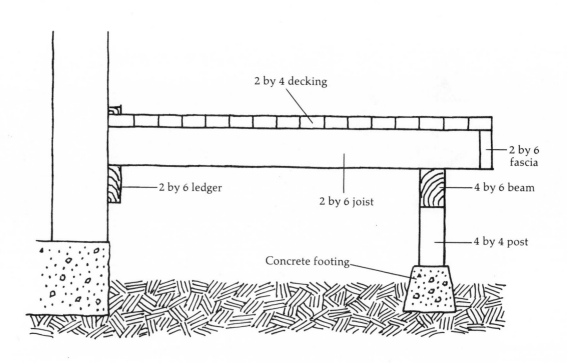

2 by 4 decking

2 by 6 fascia

2 by 6 ledger

2 by 6 joist

4 by 6 beam

4 by 4 post

Concrete footing

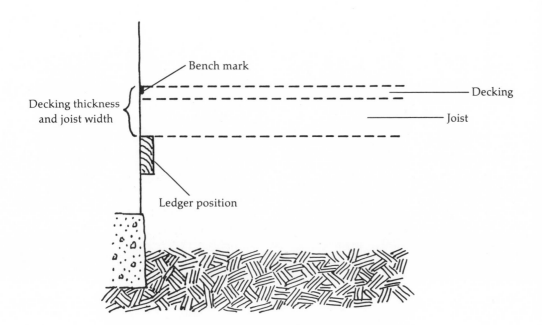

Bench mark

Decking thickness
and joist width

Decking

Joist

Ledger position

Place the ledger at the established height. The ledger, as the drawing shows, will support one end of the joists. Be sure to measure the *actual* dimensions (not nominal dimensions) of the decking thickness and joist width and compare these to the bench mark you have established. The level of the deck depends on the position of the ledger. Joist hangers may be used instead of ledgers; these are shown later in this chapter. Whatever technique you use, check local building codes to see if the technique is permitted in your community.

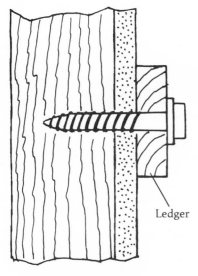

Ledger

LAG SCREW IN WOOD

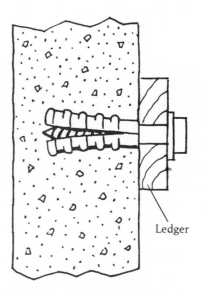

Ledger

METAL MASONRY ANCHOR

The ledger is fastened to the wall studs or other framing in the house or to the foundation of your home. The ledger may be held by lag screws, driven into framing members, or metal masonry anchors if fastening to a foundation. If you use lag screws, drill pilot holes. If you use masonry anchors, you will need a star drill to make the holes in the foundation for the anchors. If you have a portable electric drill, buy a masonry bit for the drill to make the holes in the foundation for the anchors. The electric drill method is the easier; a star drill requires a lot of pounding.

Once you establish the ledger position, you can outline the deck with a string and perimeter stakes. Measure outward from the ledger to where one corner will be. Mark the corner with a wooden stake. Now determine the other corner and mark this with a stake. To determine the squareness of these projections, measure between the stakes and the house. Now measure diagonally from the house to the opposite stakes. If the diagonals are equal, the corners of the deck are square. Sink corner posts at both outside corners, making sure they are plumb and allowing a little excess height that will be leveled off in the next step.

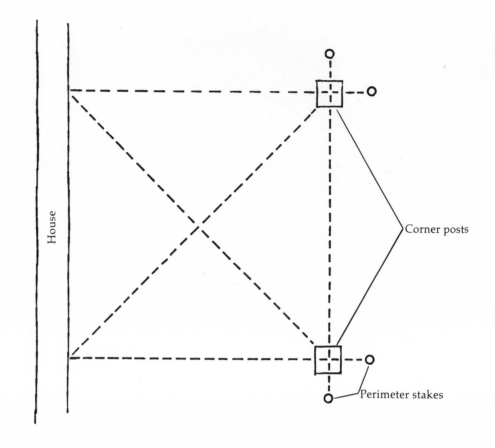

House

Corner posts

Perimeter stakes

Post lengths will probably vary since the ground is not level. You can get an accurate measurement of the posts by raising a joist, one end on the ledger, to the right level. Attach the joist temporarily to the corner post that has been set in a concrete footing. Now subtract from the post the actual depth of the beam, and mark the post so that you can saw it off to the correct size. The post must be plumb when you measure it, and you should cut it carefully so that the beam will sit squarely on the post. After you cut the post, toenail the beam to the post. Repeat this procedure for all posts; then toenail the joists to the beams.

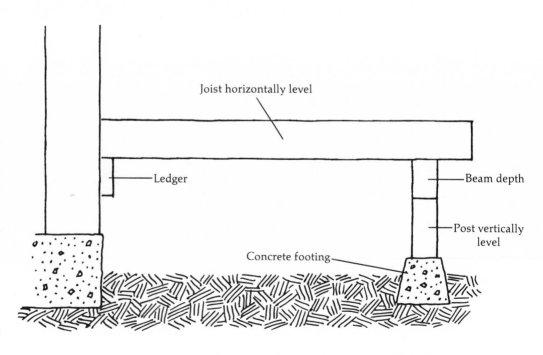

Joist horizontally level

Ledger

Beam depth

Post vertically level

Concrete footing

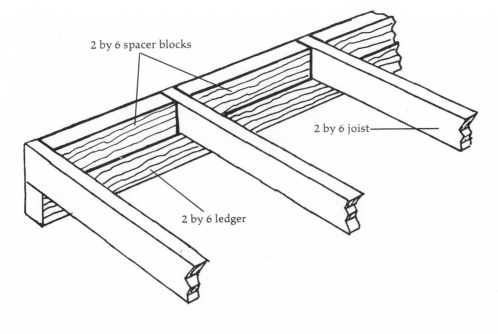

2 by 6 spacer blocks

2 by 6 joist

2 by 6 ledger

To prevent lateral movement of the joists, nail 2 by 6 spacer blocks between the joists where they rest on the ledger.

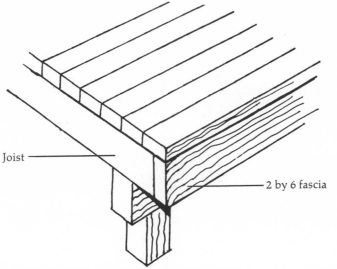

Joist

2 by 6 fascia

At the end of the deck a 2 by 6 can be nailed to the end of the joists. This serves as a fascia (trim) board.

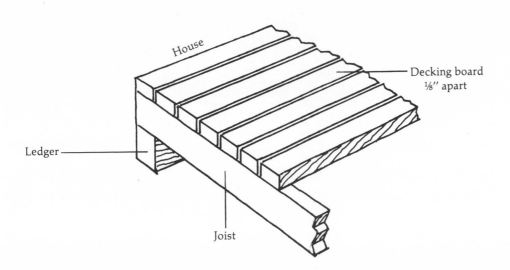

House

Decking board ⅛″ apart

Ledger

Joist

With the substructure in position, you are ready to nail the decking in position. Nail the decking parallel to the wall of the house. Allow about ⅛ inch of space between the decking boards; you might find it helpful to cut a spacing block. Use 16d stainless steel, aluminum, or hot-dipped galvanized nails to assemble your deck. Nails made from these metals cost more than regular nails; however, you will not get a staining effect (especially on redwood) with these nails.

A joist hanger is a thin piece of galvanized sheet metal in a U configuration. It may be nailed or lag-screwed to a framing member of the house. The joist is nailed between two such hangers. The joist hanger takes the place of a ledger but is not considered as substantial a support.

This view of the underside of a finished deck shows how simple the construction basics really are. The joists simply rest on the ledger at right and run perpendicular to the house. The opposite ends of the joists rest on the beam, supported by the posts, at left. The decking is nailed to the joists, parallel to the wall of the house.

Double beams are used to support an elevated deck. The diagonal bracing—2 by 4s crossed between the posts—is used to stabilize the spans. The supports for the joists are nailed or lag-screwed to the supporting posts. We recommend lag screws for more holding power.

Seat supports are double 2 by 4s or 2 by 6s nailed to the deck joists. The joists will have to extend beyond the edge of the deck for the seats, as shown.

Deck Finishes

If your deck is redwood, it may be finished in several ways or left unfinished to weather naturally. This is also true of cedar and cypress.

For any type wood that is to be finished, sand the areas where heavy dirt or other marks show. Next, wash the deck with water and a mild detergent. If there are bad stains on the wood, try using a solution of trisodium phosphate: 1 cup phosphate to 1 gallon water.

Scrub the wood with a stiff brush and hose it down with cold water. If you are going to paint or stain the deck, make sure the wood is completely dry before you apply the finish. In hot weather wait about three days before you apply the finish. If the weather is moderate or cold, wait even longer. The wood must be dry before any finish is applied to it.

A deck constructed of redwood, cedar, or cypress is most attractive left natural. However, you may want to cover the wood with a clear penetrating stain to seal the wood grain from the elements.

If the wood is fir, pine, hemlock, spruce, etc., you can use a pigmented penetrating stain to help preserve the wood. Or you can use a porch and deck enamel or exterior spar varnish for the same purpose.

Whatever finish you decide to use, consult a paint dealer for advice on the type of stain or paint best suited to your purposes, and follow his instructions for application. The paint or stain usually may be applied with a brush or roller, and standard painting procedures should be followed.

Special Features for Decks

Decks may be elaborate or as simple as your needs dictate. Some of the more traditional additions to decks—benches, fences or privacy screens, barbeque grilles, etc.—add a custom touch.

The time to add these extras is while you are constructing the deck since it is usually easier and less expensive to build now than to add on later. In this section you will find the basic framing techniques for benches and railings, along with other methods for installing fences and grilles. Be sure not to overlook the detailing of decks and patios in other chapters of this book; there you will find a potpourri of ideas that you can copy or adapt for your own project.

You do not always need to cut down trees to make way for a deck. Instead, build the deck around the trees. You must leave room for tree growth, so do not jam the headers and joists tightly against the trees, unless the tree is very small in diameter. Consult a nurseryman for information on full growth size, if you are unsure about the amount of space to leave for growth.

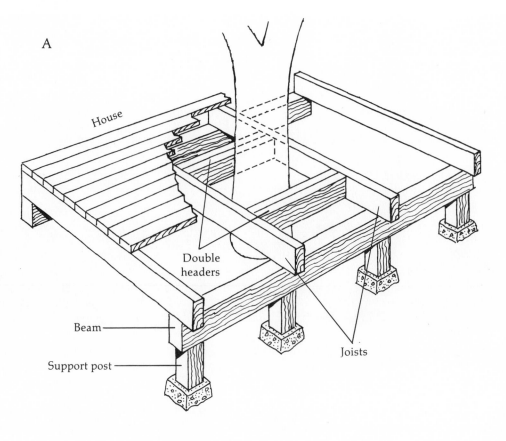

A

House

Double
headers

Beam

Support post

Joists

Joists are spaced 16 or 24 inches on center. Maintain this spacing even though you are working around a tree. If the tree will fit between two joists, brace the joists with double headers, as shown in drawing A. The headers are the same width and thickness as the joists. Nail through the joists into the header; the decking will cover the headers.

If the tree is large and will not fit between the normal joist span, construct double headers between the two closest joists; then add two short joists equal distance from each of the surrounding joists as shown in drawing B. The headers and added joists give the deck area around the tree adequate support.

Without nailing the boards in place, lay the decking around the tree. Measure and then cut with a saw those boards that will fit around the tree. Nail the decking into position.

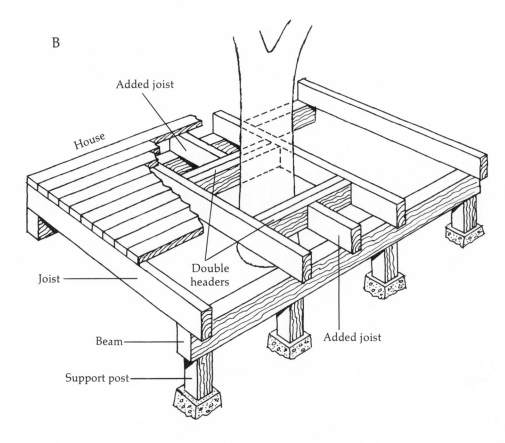

B

Added joist

House

Double
headers

Joist

Beam

Support post

Added joist

Utility-type steps to a deck are constructed the same way as basement stairsteps: two notched stringers and treads. Lay out the notches on 2- by 12-inch lumber with a carpenter's square; cut the notches with a crosscut saw or portable electric saw. Nail or toenail the stringers to the deck trim or joists. The treads are 2-inch thick lumber; the width depends on the depth of the notches. Nail the treads to the stringers with 16d hot-dipped galvanized nails, aluminum nails, or stainless steel nails.

Deck fencing or railings may be wooden or wrought iron. As with all fencing materials, you have a wide selection. The most common is wrought iron railing, which is usually fastened to posts, as shown. Fencing is either fastened to the decking or set just outside the perimeter of the decking surface.

Custom touch on railing is a wooden top rail. It is a piece of 2 by 6 dadoed (grooved) to accept the top wrought iron rail. The ends of the railing are supported by notched 2 by 4s nailed to the posts; the wooden top rail is nailed to this notched 2 by 4. This post is hollow; it is fabricated with 1 by 10s butt-joined together in a square configuration. The joints are fastened with 8d galvanized finishing nails spaced at 2-inch intervals. The post cap is a stock item at most millwork shops or stores that sell millwork.

Far left:
Floor mounting bracket for iron railing is screwed to wooden decks, as shown. The railing simply fits down into the flange. To make sure the alignment is correct, install the fencing before you drive the screws through the flange into the wooden deck.

Left:
Support posts for benches, fencing, and railings on wooden decks may be supported by galvanized brackets which retail for about $1.20 each at most hardware stores and building materials outlets. The brackets are nailed or screwed to the decking; then the posts are screwed or nailed into the bracket.

Support posts for the railing fencing may be a continuation of the deck support posts, as shown. The fencing simply attaches to these posts. In this framing, you may use iron railing, boards, fiber glass, plywood, natural fiber screening, or almost any other rigid fencing or screening. To secure the beam against the support post, lag-screw or bolt a 2 by 4 ledger strip underneath the beam.

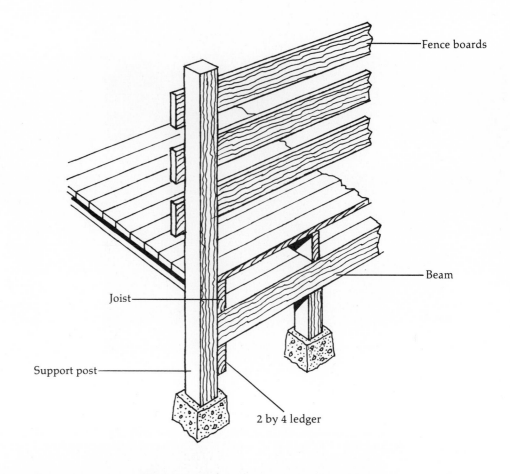

Fence boards

Beam

Joist

Support post

2 by 4 ledger

A wooden hand railing is very easy to add to your deck. The rail here is a 2 by 6 supported on one end by a 4 by 4 post and on the other end by the house structure. Additional 4 by 4 posts along the length of the span may be added for extra support, depending on the size of your deck. The railing is fastened to the post by lag screws which are counter-sunk (recessed) into the railing as shown. The top of the post has been beveled with a crosscut saw.

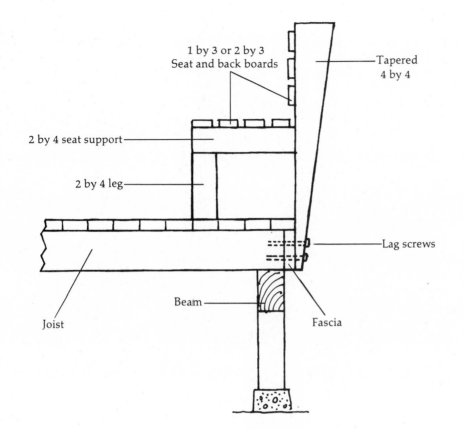

1 by 3 or 2 by 3
Seat and back boards

Tapered
4 by 4

2 by 4 seat support

2 by 4 leg

Lag screws

Joist

Beam

Fascia

A seat back for a deck bench can be constructed from a tapered 4 by 4 post fastened to the 2 by 8 or 2 by 10 fascia board and joists around the decking. Carriage bolts or lag screws are used to fasten the posts to the fascia board. Use lag screws, also, to fasten the 2 by 4 or 2 by 6 seat supports to the posts and to the legs in front. The legs may be 2 by 4s or 4 by 4s, whichever looks best. For the seat and back, use 1-inch or 2-inch boards for the best appearance.

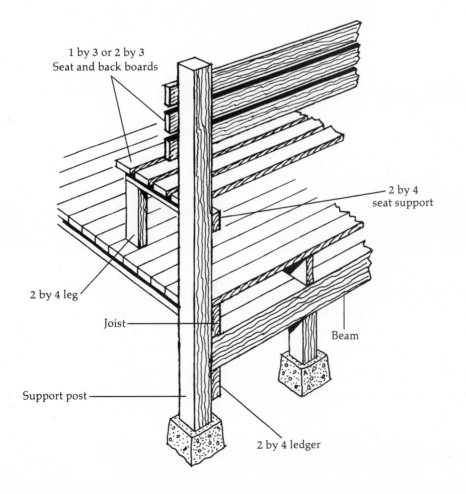

1 by 3 or 2 by 3
Seat and back boards

2 by 4
seat support

2 by 4 leg

Joist

Beam

Support post

2 by 4 ledger

A straight seat back may be an extension of the deck support posts, following the same design principle shown earlier for a deck railing. For seat supports, use 2 by 4s lag-screwed or bolted to the posts; use 2 by 4s or 4 by 4s for the seat legs. The seat back and seat may be 1-inch or 2-inch lumber. A comfortable height for the seat—from the deck surface to the seat surface—is about 18 to 20 inches. Since the seat is fastened to the support posts and the seat support, you do not have to fasten the legs to the deck. However, if you want to do so, toenail the legs to the decking or use metal brackets to support the legs. The 2 by 4 ledger strip is bolted or lag-screwed to the support post to secure the beam in position.

Barbeque grilles are popular additions to decks. A permanent support for the grille is shown here. By removing and refitting two deck boards, you can sink the grille support in concrete just as you would a fence post (see the chapter on Fences and Gates). The trick here is to locate the grille where it will be handy; consider entertaining patterns before you permanently install the grille in concrete. You can lag-screw or bolt the grille support to the decking; a special flange is manufactured for this installation. If you support the grille with a flange, it can be readily relocated.

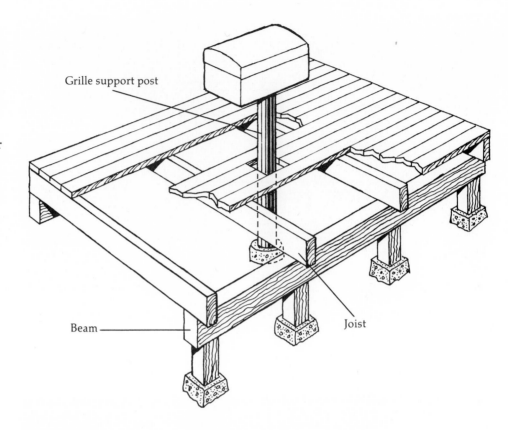

Grille support post

Beam

Joist

Deck Ideas

Very wide steps add dimension to this fairly small deck. The steps are constructed just the same as the main deck— footings, joist supports, and matching deck boards. The bench at the left is supported by the deck posts, which extend above the top deck level; the bench supports are nailed to these posts.

This two-level deck is supported by concrete footings and 4 by 4 posts. Here, one level is established and the adjoining deck surfaces are constructed to match. The perimeter of each level is faced with a 2 by 8 to cover the ends of the joist spans. The height of each unit is determined by the length of the support posts on the footings.

Wood and brick combine to make this outdoor living area an architectural success. The different levels are a series of small decks, playing off the large one attached to the house. The benches are 2 by 4s spaced with 1 by 4 strips and supported by 4 by 4 posts spiked to the decking material. The L-shape design adds sturdiness.

Screening—1 by 3s equally spaced—hides the substructure of this deck. The screening can run either vertically, as shown, or horizontally, depending on the architectural appearance you want. The stairsteps are notched out of 2 by 12 stringers and are attached to the joist framing. The posts are set in concrete, and the rails and rail caps are nailed to the posts. For step construction, see the chapter on Patios.

This simple deck design is built around a tree, instructions for which appear earlier in this section. The benches are attached to the deck-ing joists. The back rail of the bench is dadoed into the uprights; however, you could nail this backing flush onto the uprights. The back slope is about 30 degrees.

Fences and Gates

Fences and gates are as decorative as they are functional. Fences can screen a bad view and offer privacy; they can add architectural interest to your home; and fences can accent a garden planting or a special tree or garden structure. In addition, fences add an element of safety to your home—especially important if you have small children or pets that must be confined.

There are hundreds of fence and gate designs, and they may be constructed out of almost any building material available. In this chapter the choices have been narrowed to the most common styles and materials used. Basic design and construction details are included; you need only to adapt these to your particular fencing project.

Fences have three parts: 1) the fence posts, vertical members usually set in concrete that support the rails and the screening; 2) the fence rails, horizontal members that are attached to the posts and support the screening; and 3) the fence screening, which can be rails, pickets, boards and battens, or louvers.

As a general rule, it is best to keep the fence design basic and "clean." Do not clutter up the design with a lot of gimcracks and gingerbread. The fence should blend with the architecture of your home, not distract from it.

Before you get into design and actually start constructing a fence, be sure to check the building codes or ordinances in your area. It could be that local laws limit the height and design of fences in your neighborhood (especially if the fence is to enclose a swimming pool). The building codes may also specify how far back from the property line the fence must be set.

You might also check with your neighbor before building your fence. Good fences sometimes make good neighbors, but fences can also make neighbors angry. For good community relations, discuss your project with your neighbor. Who knows, he may even help you build it!

The tools you will need for constructing most wooden fences and gates include the following:

13- or 16-ounce claw hammer
Crosscut saw
Spirit level
Set of wood chisels
Flexible measuring tape
String
Carpenter's framing square or a combination square
Tile spade
Posthole digger
Screwdriver

The tools you will need for installing a chain link fence include these:

13-ounce claw hammer
Hacksaw
Heavy-duty pliers
Spirit level
Adjustable wrenches (2)
Wire cutters
Fence stretcher
Posthole digger

A fence usually has a gate. The gate should blend in with the fence design but should not look formidable. A gate should welcome your friends and neighbors and yet be sturdy enough to withstand the continual punishment from opening and closing.

Fence and Gate Materials

Fences and gates can be built from almost any type of wood. Redwood, cedar, or cypress are best, however, because these woods are rot- and insect-resistant. Redwood, cedar, and cypress will last for decades without requiring any paint or stain or much maintenance of any sort. Other woods, such as pine, spruce, hemlock—and plywood—may also be used for constructing fences and gates, but they will not withstand exposure to the weather as well as redwood, cedar, or cypress. If you do not use one of these woods for the posts, coat your posts with a wood preservative before setting them in the ground.

If you use plywood, make sure the grade is exterior type. Exterior type plywood has a special waterproof glue bond that prevents the plywood from delaminating with weather conditions. You must, however, keep the edges of the plywood sealed with penetrating stain or paint.

Redwood, cedar, and cypress lumber are more expensive than are spruce, hemlock, fir, and pine. However, the low-maintenance feature of the more expensive woods may outweigh the expense. The cost of materials will vary, depending on where you live.

If the fence and gate you plan to build will be painted, such as a gothic picket fence or a board and board fence, choose an inexpensive wood. The paint covering will help preserve the wood and will cover up any imperfections in the wood.

For an attractive fence, use any good exterior grade paint. Be sure, however, to prime all component parts of the fence before asembling the fence; then add one or two coats of paint to the primer after the fence is in place. If you do not paint or stain the fence, remember to treat the lumber with a preservative.

Posts should be set in concrete for a strong, permanent fence. Dry-mix cement is easier to use than concrete that must be mixed or concrete that must be ordered from a supplier.

Set the post that the gate is hinged to in concrete. This post must be perfectly plumb (vertically level). Make the gate at least 3 feet wide and hinge it to the post with top quality, rustproof hinges.

For fastening the fence and gate components together, aluminum or galvanized nails and/or screws are best. The hardware for the fence (hinges and latches) should be heavy-duty and weather-resistant.

Most fences are constructed with 4 by 4 posts, 2 by 4 rails, and 1-inch boards for screening. After you determine the design of the fence and gate(s) and order the materials, store the wood under cover and off the ground. Store lumber material flat; if you lean it up against a wall, the lumber may warp or bend.

Fence Design and Dimensions

There are any number of attractive fence designs. The examples that follow illustrate the most popular styles with the typical dimensions. Two gate designs are also included; the designs and dimensions are typical and can easily be adapted to fit your specific construction needs.

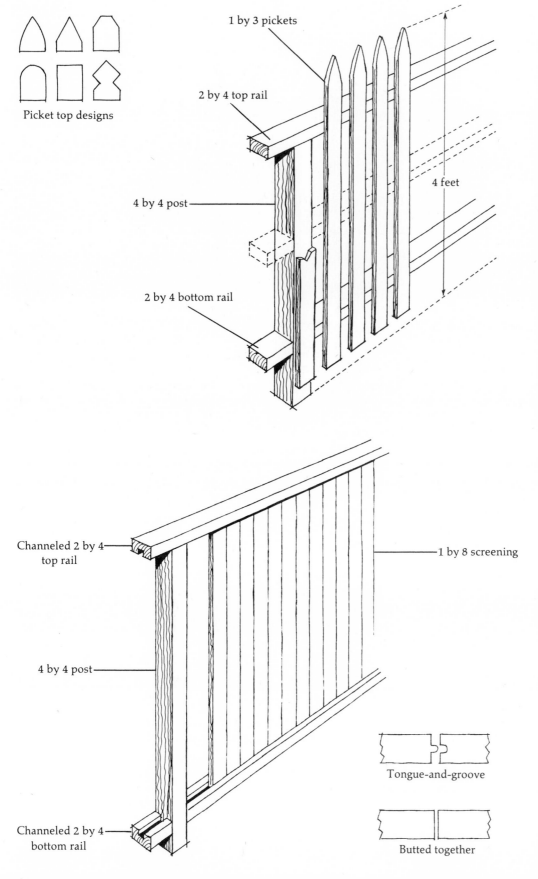

Picket top designs

1 by 3 pickets

2 by 4 top rail

4 by 4 post

2 by 4 bottom rail

4 feet

Channeled 2 by 4 top rail

4 by 4 post

Channeled 2 by 4 bottom rail

1 by 8 screening

Tongue-and-groove

Butted together

Picket fence. The pickets are usually 1 by 3 boards nailed to two 2 by 4 rails supported by 4 by 4 posts. You can often buy the pickets precut, but if the precut pickets are unavailable, cut the 1 by 3 boards to the desired shape with a combination, coping, or power saw. Smooth the cut with a plane. First make a cardboard template the exact shape you want the point to be. Use the template to cut each picket; do not use a cut picket. Transfer the design to the board and cut the board along the guidelines. Many designs are possible, some of which are shown here.

The pickets should be nailed to the rails with 8d (penny) galvanized, aluminum casing, or finishing box nails. Picket fences are quite attractive painted. Use any good exterior grade paint for this fence.

Good neighbor fence. This attractive design is called a good neighbor fence because it looks the same on both sides. The materials used can be the same as for any style fence, but the screening portion of the fence may be constructed of tongue-and-groove boards or boards simply butted together. The rails are dadoed (grooved) or channeled to accent the ends of the tongue-and-groove boards. A good neighbor fence is attractive painted, stained, or left natural.

Board and board fence. Because of the quantity of lumber needed to construct this style fence, the cost may run high. The fence, however, is easy to construct with 4 by 4 anchor posts and 2 by 4 rails. The screening may be constructed of boards of equal width or boards of two widths alternated, as shown. The components are assembled with 8d galvanized nails or aluminum nails. It is important that you build this fence in 6- to 8-foot sections since the top and bottom rails may not be perfectly straight. The rails are notched into the posts, or, more simply, they may be toenailed into the posts or supported by cleats nailed to the posts. These techniques are discussed later in this chapter. The fence may be left natural if you use redwood, cedar, or cypress wood. Be sure to treat the lumber with a wood preservative.

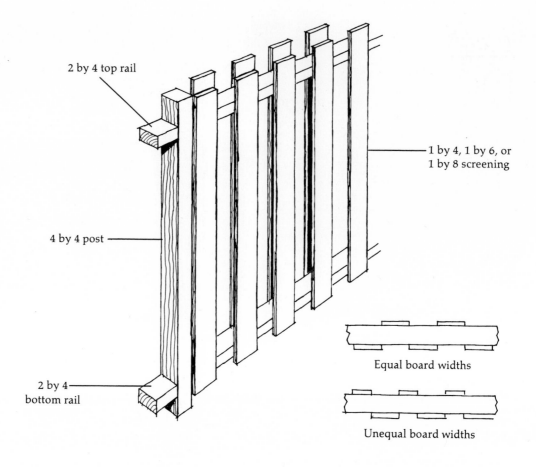

2 by 4 top rail

1 by 4, 1 by 6, or 1 by 8 screening

4 by 4 post

2 by 4 bottom rail

Equal board widths

Unequal board widths

Post and rail or crossbuck fence. The sprawling horse breeding farms in Kentucky and Tennessee have made this style fence—usually painted white—a favorite. Unless you have a pasture full of horses or cows to confine, the fence is not particularly functional. The fence usually is built in 6-foot sections, according to the dimensions shown here. Use 8d galvanized nails or aluminum nails for fasteners. Prime the wood before you assemble the component parts; then add a coat of exterior grade white paint after the fence is in place.

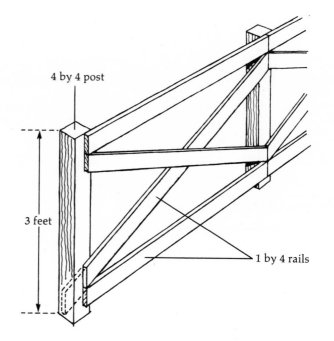

4 by 4 post

3 feet

1 by 4 rails

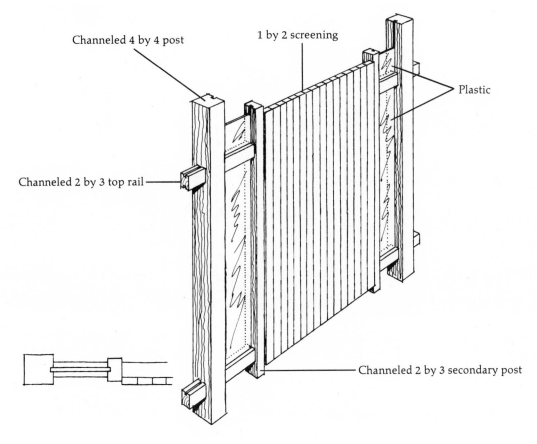

Channeled 4 by 4 post

1 by 2 screening

Plastic

Channeled 2 by 3 top rail

Channeled 2 by 3 secondary post

Redwood and plastic fence. This intriguing fence style is expensive to build because of the amount of lumber involved. The plastic is colored fiber glass and is inserted in dadoes (grooves) in the posts and rails. The fiber glass has to be specially cut for this since fiber glass usually comes in 4- by 8-foot sheets. Triangular post caps may be used effectively on this fence design; they are prefabricated and are available at a building materials outlet or from a millwork dealer. The entire unit is assembled with aluminum or galvanized nails (8d, depending on thickness). The fence is redwood, so you may want to leave the wood natural and take advantage of its weathering properties.

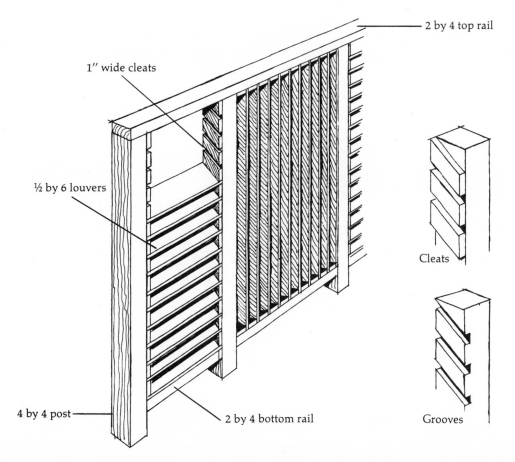

1" wide cleats

2 by 4 top rail

½ by 6 louvers

Cleats

4 by 4 post

2 by 4 bottom rail

Grooves

Alternating louvered fence. This is a difficult fence to build because the louvers are set either between cleats or in grooves, both of which must run at a 45-degree angle. If you enjoy Chinese puzzles, you will not have trouble building this fence, but it is not a weekend job. The fence is assembled with 8d galvanized or aluminum nails. The fence may be painted, stained, or left natural, depending on the wood you use. This makes a good "accent" fence; a section or two is used to highlight a garden planting or screen an unpleasant view.

Louvered fence. This fence style is not as difficult to build as the alternating louvered fence, but there are details involved in nailing the spacer blocks to the top and bottom rails. These blocks have to be perfectly aligned or the louvers will not fit properly. You can build this with a crosscut saw, but in the interest of time, a power saw is better. The fence is assembled with 8d galvanized or aluminum casing or box nails. The fence may be painted, stained, or left natural. If you choose to paint the fence, prime the wood before you assemble the fence.

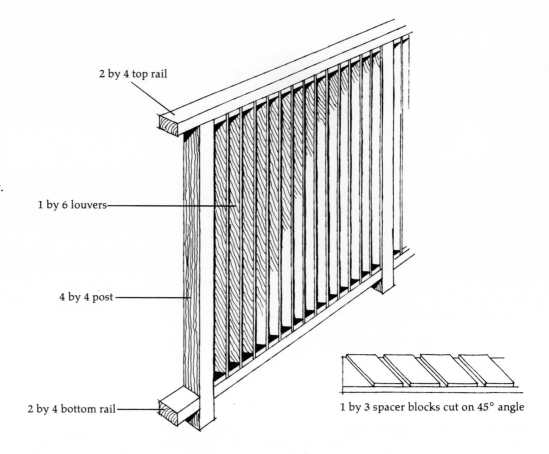

2 by 4 top rail

1 by 6 louvers

4 by 4 post

2 by 4 bottom rail

1 by 3 spacer blocks cut on 45° angle

Basketweave fence. You can usually buy this style in prefabricated 4-, 6-, and 8-foot sections, which is a bargain both in money and time spent. Whether you use the prefabricated sections or construct your own, assemble the fence sections with 8d galvanized or aluminum nails. The prefabricated sections are often stained.

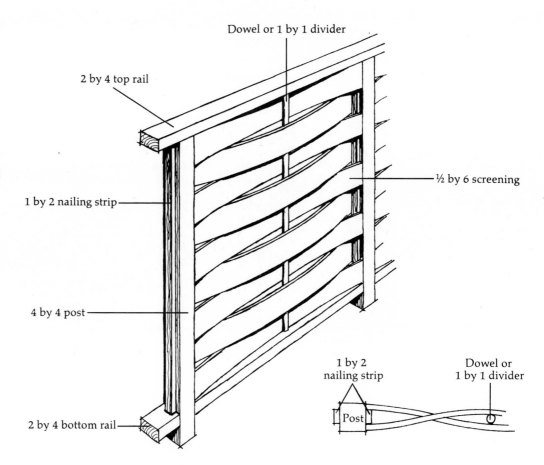

Dowel or 1 by 1 divider

2 by 4 top rail

1 by 2 nailing strip

4 by 4 post

2 by 4 bottom rail

½ by 6 screening

1 by 2 nailing strip

Post

Dowel or 1 by 1 divider

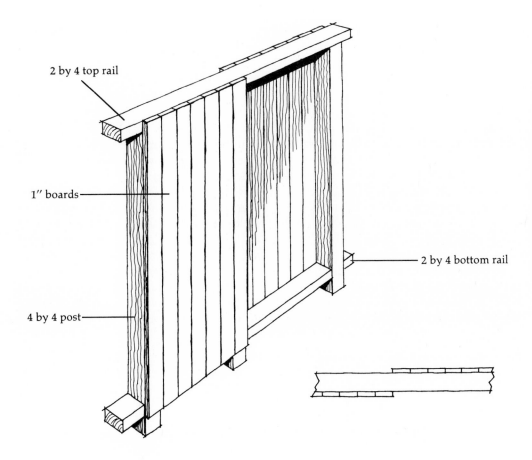

2 by 4 top rail

1″ boards

4 by 4 post

2 by 4 bottom rail

Alternating panel fence. This functional design is expensive because it takes a lot of material to build. Instead of boards, you could use grooved exterior grade plywood for the screening. This will lower the cost and will also speed up the construction time because you can nail up 4-foot wide pieces of plywood at one time, instead of nailing on 1-inch thick boards. This fence looks best painted or stained.

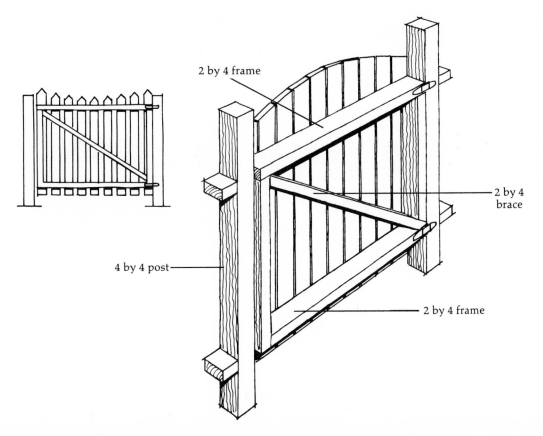

2 by 4 frame

4 by 4 post

2 by 4 brace

2 by 4 frame

Board or picket gate. A gate is really just a 3- or 4-foot wide section of fence. To withstand continual opening and closing, it is specially braced with a framework of 2 by 4s. The pickets on a gate are made in the same way as for the picket fence. The gate may take on a different look by using boards butted tightly together or spaced out, as shown here; it really depends on the fence design you choose. Caps for the posts may be added; they are precut and are available at many building material dealers. Use the best hinges and latches available to support the gate; this metal is subject to quite a bit of stress and weathering. Cheap hardware will have to be replaced on an average of every two years.

Post Setting Details

After you have laid out the fencing pattern, the first step is to set the terminal posts in the ground. Do not dig postholes in advance; set one terminal post first, and work from that point. Work by sections of fence: there is less margin for error. A section may be any length, depending on the fence design, but in most cases sections are 6- to 8-feet. Dig holes about 8 inches in diameter and about one-third the length of the post deep. If you have a lot of holes to dig, rent a power posthole digger (about $15 per day) for the job. If you do not have a lot of holes to dig, rent an auger-type digger or a clamshell-type digger.

The normal spacing between corner posts will vary from 6 to 8 feet, depending on the type fence you are building. If you have chosen a "light" fence—the framing members are lightweight boards—set the posts every 8 feet apart. If the fence will include "heavy" construction members, use 6-foot spacing since the posts will handle the weight of these members.

Remember to set all corner posts first; then dig the holes for the in-between posts as you build the fence. Otherwise, if you are a bit out of alignment with the posts, you may have to remove the posts and set them again. Any error in the original calculations will compound itself as you go: if you are off 2 inches on the first two posts, you may find the alignment is off 2 feet by the last post.

Posts may be set in the ground in three ways: in concrete, with cleats, or in tamped earth. The drawings show both the concrete and the cleat method of setting posts. Tamped earth is firmed around the post in the hole. The best method of setting posts is with concrete simply because it is easier to work with and the posts will set solid and plumb.

Whether you set the posts in concrete or in dirt, throw half a shovel full of gravel into the hole before positioning the post in the hole. The gravel will provide drainage for ground water.

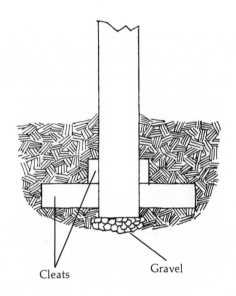

Cleats   Gravel

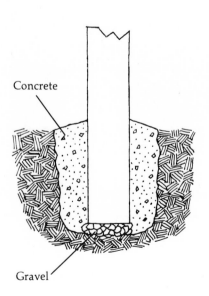

Concrete

Gravel

After the posts are positioned in the holes, pour in the cement mixture. Add water according to the instructions on the package, and stir the mixture in the hole with a stick, as shown. This makes an extremely strong mixture of concrete, and you avoid having to premix the concrete in a bucket and pour it into the hole.

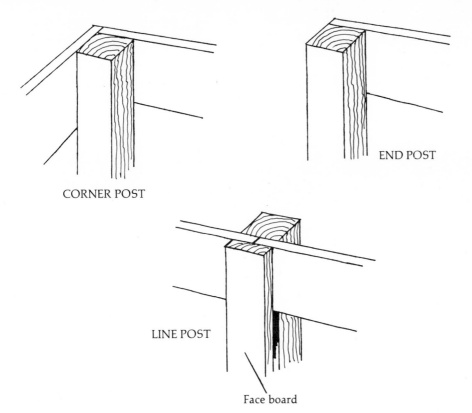

CORNER POST

END POST

LINE POST

Face board

Working in 8-foot sections of fence does not mean that the postholes will be spaced 8 feet apart. Corner, end, and gate posts are treated differently from the line posts, and the fence may be fastened to the line posts in different ways. In short, the space between a corner, end, or gate post and the first line post may vary. It is best to build one section of the fence at a time, digging the necessary holes as you proceed. The drawings here illustrate three methods in which fence sections are joined to posts.

Right:
As a guideline in setting fence posts, stretch a length of string between each set of corner posts. The string will help you align each section of fence. If your fencing plan calls for turning a corner, use the right angle technique for alignment shown later in this chapter.

Far right:
Plumb each post as you set it. Plumb the post on two sides to make sure it is vertically level. Make sure the posts are in alignment by using the string guideline.

Right:
After the posts are set, stretch the string across the top of the posts to establish the uniform height you want. Mark along the string with a square as shown. Double-check your measurements before you cut the posts to height. If you set the posts in concrete as recommended, wait 5 days before making any height cuts; this time lapse permits the concrete to harden properly.

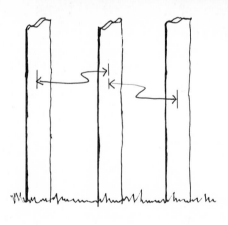

Far right:
To set the fence posts, employ one of two measuring techniques. At the top, the posts are set and spaced by measuring the given distance from the last post set, starting with a corner terminal post. On the bottom, the position of each post is determined by measuring from one corner or terminal post; in this way, if one post is slightly misplaced, the other posts are not affected. However, you should be as accurate as possible when positioning each post.

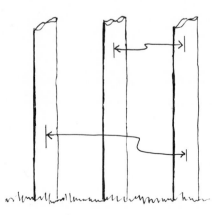

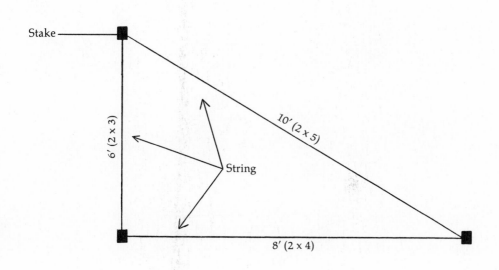

Stake

6' (2 x 3)

10' (2 x 5)

String

8' (2 x 4)

Right-angle corners with fencing are easy to construct. First, determine an approximate right angle to the base line, as shown. Measure along the perpendicular from the base line 3 feet or a multiple of 3 feet. Measure 4 feet or the same multiple of 4 feet along the established base line. The diagonal line connecting these two points will be 5 feet times the given multiple—if the corner is square. In this example, working with a multiple of 2 gives 6-, 8-, and 10-foot measurements. This is easier to calculate than trying to square a corner with a carpenter's square.

Gently sloping ground calls for "racking." First anchor the section of the fence to the end or corner post, if the fence is sectional. Once fastened securely, pull the opposite end of the section down into the position you want. When you rack a section of fence, you shorten the span slightly. You must allow for this measurement change and compensate for it as you build the fence.

Rail fences—to which rails or boards are fastened—are constructed on a gentle slope by nailing the top rail flush with the top of the corner post, then pulling the opposite end of the top rail down and nailing it to the next post, which is slightly lower. Install the bottom rail next, making sure that it slopes at the same angle as the top rail. The center rail should divide the distance between and run exactly parallel to the top and bottom rails.

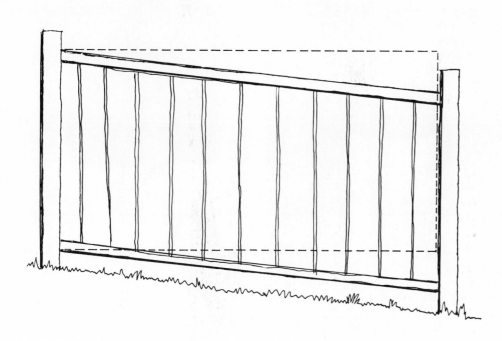

If you are building a solid or louvered fence on a very steep incline, the fence should step down the slope in sections. To align the fence properly and to ensure adequate support for the sections, it is necessary to dig a trench from point A to point B. You can construct your fence sections with a slanting bottom line to conform to the sloping ground as shown in the second drawing; a trench in this case would not be necessary.

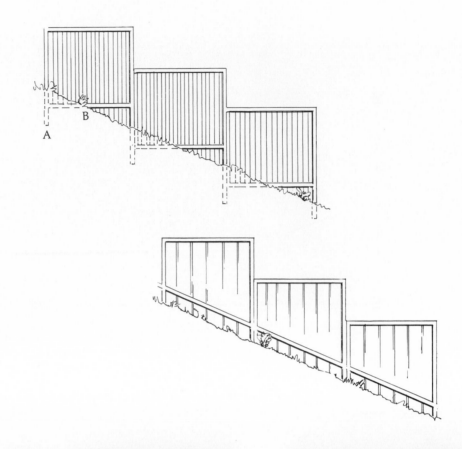

Right:
If posts must be set over concrete—use the drift pin method. First align the posts with the rest of the fence. Then scribe the outline of the bottom of the post on the concrete. Diagonally "X" this square to find the center. Make sure you double-check your alignment and measurements. Drill a hole in the concrete for the drift pin, as shown here.

Far right:
The drift pin can be a galvanized carriage bolt or a piece of reinforcing rod. Diagonally "X" the bottom of the post to find the center of the square. Drill a hole at this point to accept the pin. Drive the pin squarely into the post. Set the post down, inserting the pin into the hole. Plumb the post two ways and fasten the fence rails to it. This will hold it plumb or vertically level. The post will not move laterally from this position; you do not need to cement the drift pin into the concrete.

Wooden Gate Details

Hang all gates as you come to them. It is almost impossible to jiggle the posts after they have been set to conform to the gate. Leave about ½ inch clearance between the gate frame and the posts. Leave about 3 inches of space at the bottom of the gate so that the gate will swing properly. Consider the gate post and the gate as a single unit.

The gate shown here is fairly thick. Therefore, a standard latch will not work. The solution is an aluminum T latch that may be operated from both sides of the gate. The T drops into a hole in the concrete; the hole is slightly larger than the diameter of the aluminum rod. Galvanized steel pipe may be substituted for the aluminum.

The aluminum T latch is supported by eye screws, which are screwed into the gate member, as shown. You will need several eye screws so that the T latch will "track" properly into the hole in the concrete. To drive the eye screws, first drill a pilot hole in the wood; then insert the eye screws and drive them flush with the wood, using an old screwdriver for leverage.

Joining Techniques

For the most part, there are three basic joints used in constructing wooden fences: 1) where the rails fit on the posts, 2) where the screening fits on the rails, and 3) where a cap board is used.

Fence joints are very simple in construction. The type of joint you choose really depends on what type of woodworking equipment you have.

Some joints are stronger than others.

For example, a butt joint is not as strong as a dado joint, but a butt joint is easier to make. Generally, the strength of the joints is important when building fences, but the main strength should come from the anchor or support posts, which are set in concrete. The rest of the fence structure is built on these posts.

This section shows a potpourri of fence joints that you can easily copy. Pick the joint that best suits your fence design, the tools you have, and your skills.

Lap corner or line post joint. The horizontal rail simply laps against the post and is fastened to the post with 16d (penny) nails. Lag screws may also be used to secure this joint; they are sturdier but are also more expensive and more time-consuming to drive. In most fence installations, nails are the best fasteners because you do not need the strength lag screws provide.

Butt line post joint with a board batten over the joint. The horizontal rail laps halfway across the post and is fastened to the post with nails. The next rail butts against the first. The batten is usually a 1 by 4 nailed over the joint to conceal it. However, this is a refinement in design, and the board is not really needed for structural support. Rails may be nailed flush with the tops of anchor posts or set below the tops of anchor posts, depending on the design of the fence.

Butted corner post joint. Top, middle, and bottom rails are all fastened to the post in the same manner. The trick here is to have the ends of the rails cut square so that there is no mismatching where the rails overlap. The rails may be fastened to the post with 16d galvanized casing or box nails or aluminum nails or lag screws.

Far left:
Butted top rail joint on a line post. The sections of rail should "split" the width of the post for best support. The ends of the rails should also be square so that both butt tightly against each other. This is a very strong joint since all the shear (downward pressure) is supported by the post. To fasten the rails to the post, use 16d galvanized casing nails or aluminum nails.

Left:
Post, top rail, and cap. This unit goes together in butt joints: the rail is nailed to the post; then the cap is nailed to the rail. The purpose of the cap is partially design, but it also adds a great deal of strength if you let the cap cross posts where rails meet and let the ends of the cap meet over posts where the rail is continuous. The cap also serves as a rain drain to divert rain and snow off the rails, posts, and screening below. Use 8d galvanized or aluminum nails for assembling this joint.

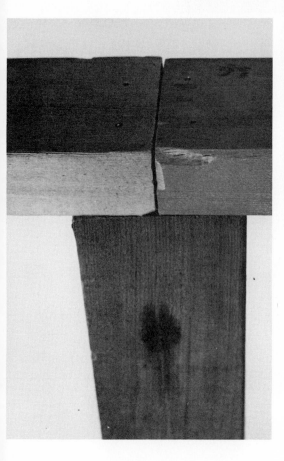

Right:
Rail butted against post and toenailed. This is a weak joint used mostly on the bottom and middle rails of a fence; the joint is usually adequate for most fence installations. The secret to a stronger joint is to have the end of the rail square so that it fits snugly against the post. 10d or 16d galvanized or aluminum nails are recommended.

Far right:
Middle rail dadoed (notched) into end or line posts and nailed. This is a tough joint to make if you do not have a power saw and dado blades. However, you can make this joint with a crosscut saw and chisel and hammer by cutting into the wood the thickness of the rail and then chiseling out the wood to make the dado or notch. This is a strong joint since the shear (downward weight) is supported by the posts. The joint is toenailed from the top and/or bottom with 8d galvanized or aluminum nails.

Middle rail supported by a 2 by 2 cleat nailed to the post. A cleated joint is a strong joint—almost as strong as a dadoed (notched) joint. The cleated joint is easy to make; the trick is to make sure the length of the cleat matches the width of the post and rail. Fasten this joint with 16d galvanized casing or aluminum nails through the cleat into the post. Then nail at an angle through the rail into the post. Since there is a danger of splitting the wood, drill pilot holes smaller than the diameter of the nails.

Butt joint on the top, middle, or bottom rail. This is basically a weak joint, but it may be strong enough to handle lightweight screening. The rail members are toenailed to the posts.

Far left:
Mitered top rail at a corner post. Both rails are cut at a 45-degree angle so that they butt perfectly across the corner post. This is a fairly strong joint, but, more importantly, it is a good-looking joint—smooth and even. Simply nail the pieces to the top of the post with 16d galvanized or aluminum nails. If the miter is somewhat out of line, pull the miter together by nailing through the edges of the 2 by 4 members. You should drill pilot holes for the nails, since the wood may split.

Left:
Corner post with blocks supporting panels. The width of the blocks or long strips between which the panels are sandwiched depends on the width of the panels and the width of the posts you are using. This really is the technique to use if you do not have a power saw with dado blades. The blocks actually form the dado or groove for you; the panels (or rails) fit between the blocks. Toenail the panels to the blocks or strips with 8d galvanized or aluminum nails. Not much support is needed since the top and bottom rails of the fence will carry the weight. The blocks or strips simply anchor the panels so that they are stable laterally.

Installing Chain Link Fencing

Chain link fencing is used more for safety or security than wood-fencing counterparts, which are more decorative. But chain link fencing does not have to be prisonlike; it may be painted or interwoven with strips. As is true when installing any fencing, there are special rules to follow when installing a chain link fence.

To set up the job, first determine the location of the end, corner, and gate posts. Mark these positions with stakes and stretch a string between them. Where the lines intersect, locate the terminal posts, as shown in the following drawing.

All posts should be set 6 inches or more inside the boundary of your property line. This could save you from the agonies of a lawsuit later. To be safe, check your local building codes about fencing.

Following the charts in this section, first lay out your chain link fencing job on graph paper so that you can see exactly where each post will go and how much material you will need for the job. Do not order material until you are certain what the measurements are. This preparation time can save quite a bit of money in the long run.

First, make sure that the centers of each post are aligned by using the stretched string guideline described earlier. Space the posts according to the chart. If your lot is odd sized and you figure an irregular measurement, try to put the shortest piece of fencing near a corner post or gate. In this way the short piece will not show as much.

Corner posts may need two diagonal braces for strength. This is not always the case, however; use your own judgment when the posts are set. End and gate posts always have one diagonal brace.

Line Post Spacing for Chain Link Fencing

Space	Set Post Apart	Space	Set Post Apart	Space	Set Post Apart	Space	Set Post Apart
30 ft.	10 ft.	56 ft.	9 ft. 4 in.	81 ft.	9 ft.	107 ft.	9 ft. 8 in.
31 ft.	7 ft. 9 in.	57 ft.	9 ft. 6 in.	82 ft.	9 ft. 1 in.	108 ft.	9 ft. 9 in.
32 ft.	8 ft.	58 ft.	9 ft. 8 in.	83 ft.	9 ft. 3 in.	109 ft.	9 ft. 10 in.
33 ft.	8 ft. 3 in.	59 ft.	9 ft. 10 in.	84 ft.	9 ft. 4 in.	110 ft.	10 ft.
34 ft.	8 ft. 6 in.	60 ft.	10 ft.	85 ft.	9 ft. 6 in.	111 ft.	9 ft. 3 in.
35 ft.	8 ft. 9 in.	61 ft.	8 ft. 8 in.	86 ft.	9 ft. 7 in.	112 ft.	9 ft. 4 in.
36 ft.	9 ft.	62 ft.	8 ft. 10 in.	87 ft.	9 ft. 8 in.	113 ft.	9 ft. 5 in.
37 ft.	9 ft. 3 in.	63 ft.	9 ft.	88 ft.	9 ft. 9 in.	114 ft.	9 ft. 6 in.
38 ft.	9 ft. 6 in.	64 ft.	9 ft.	89 ft.	9 ft. 10 in.	115 ft.	9 ft. 7 in.
40 ft.	10 ft.	65 ft.	9 ft. 3 in.	91 ft.	9 ft. 2 in.	116 ft.	9 ft. 8 in.
41 ft.	8 ft. 2 in.	66 ft.	9 ft. 5 in.	92 ft.	9 ft. 2 in.	117 ft.	9 ft. 9 in.
42 ft.	8 ft. 5 in.	67 ft.	9 ft. 7 in.	93 ft.	9 ft. 3 in.	118 ft.	9 ft. 10 in.
43 ft.	8 ft. 6 in.	68 ft.	9 ft. 8 in.	94 ft.	9 ft. 5 in.	119 ft.	9 ft. 10 in.
44 ft.	8 ft. 9 in.	69 ft.	9 ft. 10 in.	95 ft.	9 ft. 6 in.	120 ft.	10 ft.
45 ft.	9 ft.	70 ft.	10 ft.	96 ft.	9 ft. 7 in.	121 ft.	9 ft. 3 in.
46 ft.	9 ft. 2 in.	71 ft.	8 ft. 9 in.	97 ft.	9 ft. 7 in.	122 ft.	9 ft. 4 in.
47 ft.	9 ft. 5 in.	72 ft.	9 ft.	98 ft.	9 ft. 8 in.	123 ft.	9 ft. 5 in.
48 ft.	9 ft. 7 in.	73 ft.	9 ft. 2 in.	99 ft.	9 ft. 9 in.	124 ft.	9 ft. 6 in.
49 ft.	9 ft. 9 in.	74 ft.	9 ft. 3 in.	100 ft.	10 ft.	125 ft.	9 ft. 7 in.
50 ft.	10 ft.	75 ft.	9 ft. 4 in.	101 ft.	9 ft. 2 in.	126 ft.	9 ft. 8 in.
51 ft.	8 ft. 6 in.	76 ft.	9 ft. 6 in.	102 ft.	9 ft. 3 in.	127 ft.	9 ft. 9 in.
52 ft.	8 ft. 8 in.	77 ft.	9 ft. 7 in.	103 ft.	9 ft. 4 in.	128 ft.	9 ft. 10 in.
53 ft.	8 ft. 10 in.	78 ft.	9 ft. 9 ih.	104 ft.	9 ft. 5 in.	129 ft.	9 ft. 10 in.
54 ft.	9 ft.	79 ft.	9 ft. 10 in.	105 ft.	9 ft. 6 in.		
55 ft.	8 ft. 2 in.	80 ft.	10 ft.	106 ft.	9 ft. 7 in.		

Post Height Chart

Fence Height	Terminal Post Height Above Ground	Line Post Height Above Ground
36 in.	38 in.	34 in.
42 in.	44 in.	40 in.
48 in.	50 in.	46 in.
60 in.	62 in.	58 in.
72 in.	74 in.	70 in.

Post positions and height of the posts are important. This chart will help you determine the height, according to the lengths of the posts you buy.

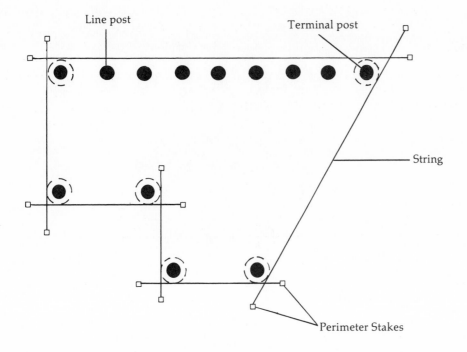

Line post

Terminal post

String

Perimeter Stakes

After positioning the terminal posts, align the line posts with the centers of the corner and gate posts. The outside faces of the line posts should be about ¼ inch inside the string stretched between the outside of the terminal posts. Terminal and corner posts should be set so that the tops of the posts extend 2 inches higher than the screening. Line posts, however, must be set so that the tops of the line posts are 2 inches below the screening height. To make sure the precut posts are buried to the correct depth, mark the posts with chalk where the ground line should hit.

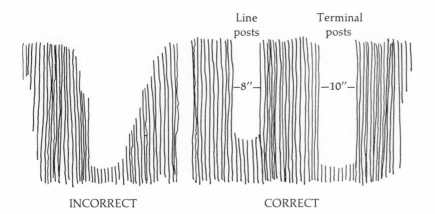

Line posts

Terminal posts

—8″—   —10″—

INCORRECT   CORRECT

Dig all post holes for chain link fence so that the sides are straight. The bottom of the hole should be as large as the top of the hole. Mix the concrete for setting: 1 part cement, 2 parts sand, and 4 parts gravel. The mixture should be "heavy"—not too much water.

Tension bands are attached to terminal posts. To fasten the screening to the tension bands, unroll the screening along the fence line; then thread the tension bar through the end of the screening and the tension bands (A). Center the bar vertically on the terminal post. Tighten the bolts on the tension bands.

To attach the screening to the opposite terminal post, hook the stretcher around the opposite terminal post and stretcher bar and stretch the screening (B). Do not put too much tension on the wire. When the screening is tight, cut it to the correct length by unscrewing one picket (C). Thread the tension bar through the end of the screening and the tension bands. Tighten the bolts and release the tension.

Gates require special consideration. You must complete the full run of a chain link fence before hanging the gates. First attach the gate hinges. Put the top hinge upside down so that the gate cannot be lifted off the pins. Loosen the female hinges on the gate frame and slip them onto the male hinges attached to the post. Allow the hinges to make a full swing of the gate. Adjust the gate height with a hammer while tightening the nuts. The center drop rod for double swing gates is installed after the gates have been installed. Fasten the catch to the opposite post to engage a spring latch on the framework of the gate. If you install a fork latch, you do not need the spring catch.

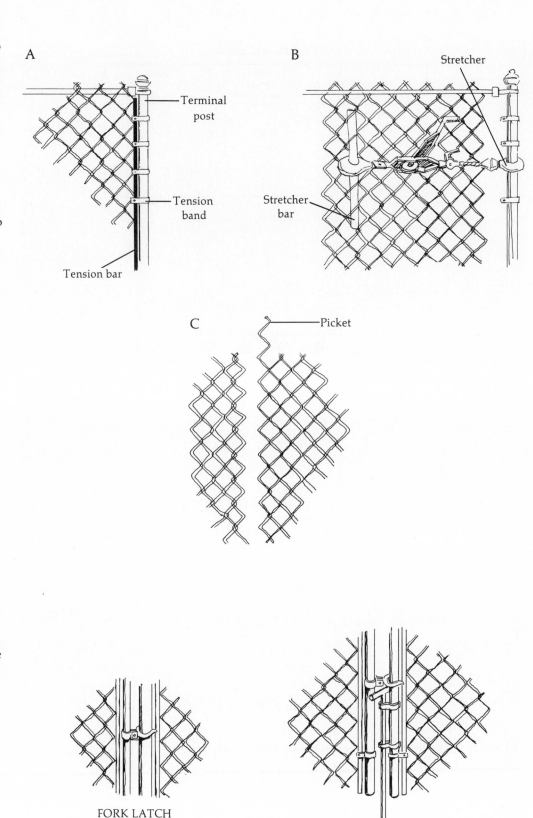

A

Terminal post

Tension band

Tension bar

B

Stretcher

Stretcher bar

C

Picket

FORK LATCH

CENTER DROP ROD

Fencing Ideas

Board and batten fence uses a combination of center or anchor posts and rails, to which the boards and battens are nailed. The brick piers shown here add support to the fence but they are often used for architectural purposes only.

Chain link fence is "decorated" by inter-weaving plastic strips through the screening. Different colored strips give the fence a checkered appearance, as well as offering privacy to the homeowner.

Right:
Plain board fence is like the one Tom Sawyer's friends painted. It is simply a series of boards butted together and nailed to rails. The rails are attached to center or anchor posts. A 1 by 6 board tops off the fence, forming a decorative feature and providing a rain cap for the fence boards.

Far right:
Grapestake fence is a series of rustic picket poles set tightly together. The fence is supported by a firmly set center or anchor post set every 6 to 8 feet of running fence. Rails are used to support the stake on the back side of the fence; the rails are nailed to the center posts.

Louvered fence really has a combination of design: louvers, straight horizontal boards, and a smart horizontal top cap. The boards are dadoed into the post members, which are set on concrete piers held by a drift pin.

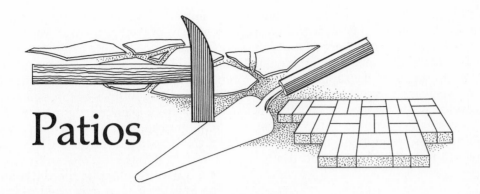

Patios

Patios are generally constructed from "hard" materials such as concrete, flagstone, and bricks. Patios may also be constructed from wood in much the same manner as you would build a deck. Although deck construction is explained in a separate chapter, instructions on how to build a wooden patio are included here.

Building a patio from concrete or brick or flagstone is hot and heavy work. These materials are heavy, and it takes a lot of muscle to get them into the position you want them to be in. On the other hand, there is nothing very complicated technically in working with these materials. In addition, you can often build your patio in sections, which gives you a rest period from weekend to weekend. Brick and flagstone may be set piece by piece so that there is no hurry involved.

Patio Design Considerations

Patios may assume almost any configuration: square, round, rectangular, or freeform.

To help you decide on your particular patio design, evaluate the following important considerations:

- Size. This probably will depend on the size of your lot and your budget.
- Location. Your patio should be part of the house; therefore, the location of doors and windows in relationship to the patio is important. Of equal importance are traffic patterns from the house to the patio and from the patio to the garden, garden structures, garages, carports, and street.

A patio with a southern exposure will be in the sun year-round. A patio facing east will be in shadow in the afternoon—an important consideration if you plan to entertain outdoors in the evening. A patio facing west will receive the late afternoon sun. A patio facing north will rarely be in the sun, particularly if it is right up against the house. Fences or trees screening a patio may also affect the amount of sunlight the patio area receives.

Concrete Patios

There are three basic steps in laying a concrete patio: 1) grade (earth) work and assembling the forms, 2) placing the concrete, and 3) finishing the concrete and stripping the forms.

If you decide to order ready-mixed concrete from a supplier (a good idea because it is easier to handle this material than it is to mix it yourself), plan for a lot of fast action and have a couple of friends handy to help you spread the ready-mixed concrete in the forms.

Ready-mixed concrete costs about $30 per yard, depending on the area in which you live. There is usually a 3- to 4-yard minimum order; if your job should call for less than 3 yards of concrete, you will have to pay for the minimum 3- or 4-yard order.

If you decide to mix your own concrete, you will need a cement mixer or a large mortar box, which you can construct from plywood. The cost to rent a cement mixer is about $18 per day, which is much more reasonable than buying one. A mortar box has approximately 6-inch sides on a 4 by 8 rectangular piece of exterior grade plywood. The box is fastened together with 8d galvanized or finishing nails. A mortar box will cost about $15 to build; plan to junk it after the project.

To work with concrete, you will need these tools:

13- or 16-ounce claw hammer
Crosscut saw
Spirit level
Carpenter's square
String
Steel finishing trowel (if you want a smooth concrete finish)
Wooden float
Edging tool
Dividing tool (if the concrete will be divided)
Square-nose shovel
Bull float (which you can make yourself)
Wire cutters or bolt cutters or a hacksaw
You will also need the following:
Wire or mesh or reinforcing rod
Screed
Stakes

Preparing the ground

Concrete patios must be designed with drainage in mind. All concrete patios should be constructed on a pitch or slope of ¼ inch per running foot of surface. The first step in preparing the area for your patio is to place the perimeter stakes around the area to be covered. If a strip of concrete is required—such as for a walkway—you also can use perimeter stakes with a string stretched between the stakes. This simply marks the area in which you will be working.

Remove all loose debris from the area and get rid of tree and shrub roots and grass and leaves. (Note that in several photographs in this chapter we have not removed the grass. This is for illustrative purposes; form outlines become clearer.)

If you have planned your patio for sloping ground, you may have to grade the area, removing dirt from the high side and moving it to the low side of the area. This is called leveling. If the difference in levels is great, you may need to construct a retaining wall. (See Retaining Walls chapter.) If you have quite a lot of dirt to move, it is wise to hire an earthmoving specialist for the job. The area on which the concrete will be placed should be as level as possible and the earth packed or tamped as firmly as possible. You may need to use sand, gravel, crushed stone, or slag for final grading. However, the layer of grade fill should not be more than 4 inches thick. Should you not be able to compact the fill tightly, discard the fill, level the earth as much as possible, and place the concrete directly over the undisturbed earth. This will form a better base.

Sandy soil and porous soil drain well. You do not need a sand, stone, or gravel base. However, if the soil is clay—or especially compact—you should have a drainage base. Lay about a 2-inch layer of sand or gravel on the area.

Building concrete forms

Forms may be boards, dimension lumber, plywood, and, if curved, tempered hardboard. For most patios, walkways, and driveways, 1 by 4s or 1 by 5s may be used. Or you can cut plywood to this measurement. If you have scrap 2 by 6s available, these may be used for forms; the heavier lumber is actually preferred for some step forms.

You will also need stakes to hold the forms in position. The stakes may be scrap boards sharpened on one end so that the stakes may be easily driven into the ground.

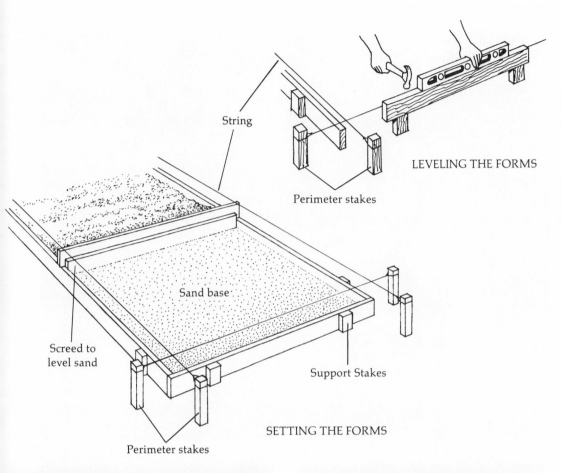

String

LEVELING THE FORMS

Perimeter stakes

Sand base

Screed to level sand

Support Stakes

SETTING THE FORMS

Perimeter stakes

Concrete forms are set according to this diagram unless curves are involved. String is tied to the perimeter stakes and leveled. The forms are then leveled from these string lines. The string simply serves as a guideline; if the project is small, you do not need perimeter stakes and guidelines. Level the forms as you go. The base (sand, gravel, etc.) is spread inside the forms after they are set; the base is leveled with a screed, shown later in this chapter.

Far left:
Stakes hold the forms in place so that the forms do not bend when the concrete is placed inside the forms. Space the stakes about every 3 feet and drive the stakes *below* the top edge of the forms. *This is a must;* the top edge of the form boards are used to level the concrete with a screed. If the stakes project above the top edge of the form boards, the concrete cannot be leveled properly.

Left:
Level and nail the forms to the stakes from the inside face of the forms into the stakes. Use two or three 6d box nails for this. Continually check the level of the forms and how the forms match the string guidelines. Remember that the string guidelines help establish the proper drainage pitch, about ¼ inch per running foot of surface.

To reinforce the forms, drive stakes diagonally against the vertical stakes and the ground, as shown. These stakes generally do not have to be nailed since they are tightly wedged in position. Pointed stakes make driving them into the ground less difficult.

Right:
If the patio will be divided—in quarters for example—and the forms are to be left in the concrete after the concrete surface has been finished, assemble the form joints as shown. Cut the ends of the forms (usually 1 by 4s, 2 by 4s, or 2 by 6s) so that the ends are perfectly square. Butt the ends of the cross boards (which are shorter) against the faces of the longer boards, which span the length or width of the patio. Toenail these cross pieces to the longer lengths of material. When you finish, you will have an "egg-crate" configuration. Use redwood, cedar, or cypress.

Far right:
Wire or mesh is used to reinforce the concrete. You may also use reinforcing rods; however, for do-it-yourself projects, the mesh is easier to handle. The wire comes in rolls usually 6 feet wide. Cut the wire with wire cutters to fit the concrete forms. Position the wire about 2 inches from the inside surface of the forms and overlap the mesh within the forms about 4 to 6 inches. As the concrete is placed in the forms, the wire will be lifted with a steel rake to about half the depth of the concrete—or 2 inches.

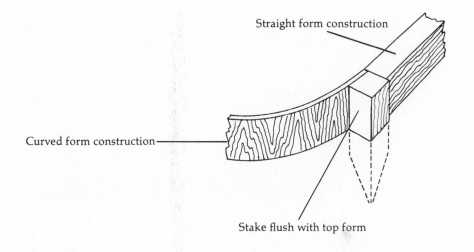

Straight form construction

Curved form construction

Stake flush with top form

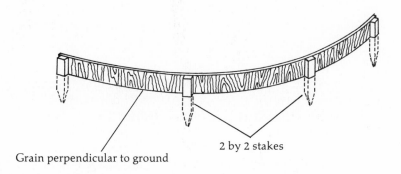

Grain perpendicular to ground

2 by 2 stakes

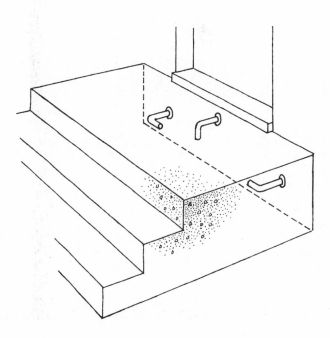

To form curves, the forms must have a smooth inner face. If the curve will be fairly short, use ¼-inch plywood or ¼-inch tempered hardboard. Use a 2 by 2 or a 2 by 4 stake where the plywood or hardboard meets the standard form.

Where long curves are involved, cut the plywood so that the grain of the plywood will be perpendicular to the ground. Position 2 by 2 stakes at 1½-foot intervals along the curved form. You may be able to use 1 by 4 boards to form long curves. If this is the case, use 2 by 2 stakes at 3-foot intervals to hold the forms firmly in position. To avoid "splicing" the forms, always use the longest piece of board you can buy.

Concrete steps are tied into the foundation of a house with reinforcing rods. To insert the rods into the foundation, drill holes for the rods with a star drill or masonry bit in a portable electric drill. Cement the rods into the foundation with epoxy cement. The rods are bent on the other end, as shown. The concrete is placed in the steps in layers. Puddle (spade) each layer and tamp the layer before you place the next layer. However, do not let each individual layer harden before you place the next layer on top of it. Steps should be furnished with a rough texture. Use a float or broom finish, as explained elsewhere in this chapter. Special metal inserts which have a non-slip surface are also available for steps.

Forming for steps requires several procedures. First, the forms must be rigid; concrete placed within thin forms will cause the forms to bulge. The end forms may be A-C grade exterior plywood with the A side facing the concrete. This way, any imperfections in the wood will not be transferred to the concrete. Nail the riser forms to the outside of the plywood side forms; this makes stripping easier. The technique shown here is 2 by 8 rectangles, each shorter in width than the one below to form the treads and risers of the steps. Make these forms from 2-inch thick lumber; the width of the lumber, of course, depends on the height you want the risers to be, but 2 by 8s are considered standard. Make sure the forms are well braced at the sides; the thrust of the concrete inside the forms can cause the forms to slide. Also, if you wish to install railings, make sure the railing attachments are embedded in the concrete before the concrete hardens. Allow about ¼-inch slope on each tread—back to front— for proper drainage.

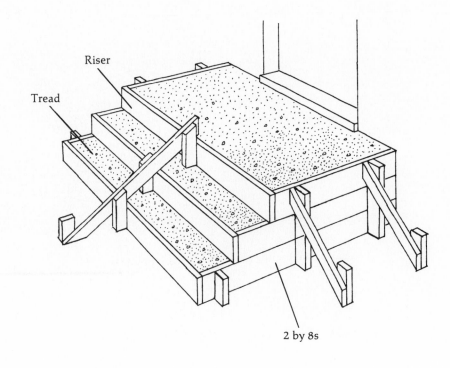

Riser

Tread

2 by 8s

Placing the concrete

As pointed out earlier in this chapter, it is best to order ready-mixed concrete for large projects such as a patio or walk or driveway. You will probably pay a little more for this ready-mixed concrete, but it will save you plenty in time and hard work. If you decide to mix your own, the details involved are explained later in this chapter.

Ready-mixed concrete requires a lot of fast action once the concrete truck arrives. Because you do have to work rapidly, it is important to be prepared.

Concrete truck drivers are a fairly patient lot, but they do not like to spend time watching you build last-minute forms or round-up your helpers by telephone.

Study the following checklist *before* the truck arrives:

☐ Have you obtained all building permits needed?

☐ Are all forms in position and are the forms sturdy and workable?

☐ Do you have extra stakes available in the event a form starts to bulge or sag when the concrete is placed?

☐ Is the reinforcing mesh in position?

☐ Is the soil extremely sandy or dry? If so, hose down the soil in the forms before the concrete is placed. This will prevent the water in the concrete from being absorbed too rapidly into the ground. You may want to cover the ground between forms with polyfilm or roll roofing to prevent water from escaping.

☐ Are all tools assembled and handy?

☐ Do you have a wheelbarrow handy? Truck concrete chutes extend only 17 feet and turn only 180 degrees. If the distance is greater than this, you will have to wheelbarrow the concrete to the forms.

☐ Are overhead wires out of the way so that the truck may enter your property? If not, contact the power and telephone companies.

☐ Are gates and fences removed so that the truck may be driven directly to the project?

☐ Do you have two friends available to help scoop and distribute the concrete mixture as it is placed? The driver of the truck will direct the cement chute; you and your friends will have to distribute the concrete coming out of the chute.

The flow of concrete down the truck chute and into the forms is controlled by the driver. Have the driver discharge a small amount of concrete at first. If you feel the mixture is too dry, the driver will hose more water into the turning mixing drum. The mixture should flow down the chute and off your shovel, but it should not be runny. The driver will help you with this decision. The driver will continue placing the concrete as you and your helpers distribute it within the forms. Try to make the distribution as even as possible. After all the concrete is in the forms, "spade" the concrete by digging the shovel into the concrete. Give the corners and edges of the forms extra attention so that all voids are filled.

Strike or screed the top of the concrete level with the top edges of the forms. This is a job for two people. A good strike is a length of 2 by 4 lumber with a straight edge. The strike should be about 3 feet longer than the width of the project. Use a lateral see-saw motion as you move the strike. If concrete builds up in front of the strike, have a helper shovel the mixture out of your way. Use the excess concrete to fill holes that may have been left behind the strike. When you have gone across the expanse, turn the strike 90 degrees (if possible) and repeat the process. When you are finished, the concrete should be level with the tops of the forms and all holes should be evenly filled. If not, repeat the screeding.

Right:
Bull float the surface of the concrete immediately after the surface has been struck. The bull float smooths and levels the concrete more exactly than the strike. However, the concrete must be leveled with a strike first; do not try to level the surface with just a bull float. Bull floats are used where a darby (float without a long handle) will not reach.

Far right:
Work the float in a see-saw motion with the bottom of the tool flat against the concrete surface. Then raise the darby or the float so that it rests mainly on one edge or side, just slightly off the concrete. Now, smooth the concrete with the leading edge of the tool. As you work these floats (bull float, darby), do not overdo it; too much floating can damage the surface of the concrete. The trick is to level and smooth the surface; then stop. Striking and floating must be completed before water from the concrete mixture starts to form on the surface of the concrete.

Missed any spots? After the initial floating you may see a spot you have missed which cannot be reached with a bull float or darby. Reach the spot by laying a piece of plywood or hardboard on the concrete surface and kneeling on this board to make repairs. The wood will make a slight indentation in the concrete. Move the board back as you move off the surface, smoothing out the indentations as you go.

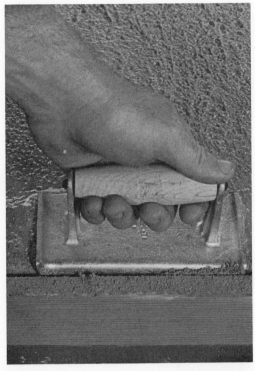

Far left:
With a trowel, slice the concrete between the inside face of the forms and the concrete. A finishing trowel may be long enough to reach the depth of the form. If not, use a pointed trowel. The idea here is to create a smooth edge along the concrete after the forms have been removed.

Left:
An edging tool is used to make the edges of the concrete around the forms slightly rounded. Simply run the edger along the inside top edges of the forms, which serve as a guide for the edger. The trick here is not to use too much pressure on the edger so that you do not leave a groove from the edger on the surface of the concrete.

Far left:
Control joints prevent the concrete from cracking after the concrete has hardened. Placing a control joint every four feet—the width and length of the patio—is desirable. Or the patio may be halved or quartered with control joints. To make a control joint, use a straightedge (1 by 4 or 2 by 4) that spans the width (or length) of the project. Check the straightedge to be sure it is square with the forms. Now, with the edge of a trowel, slice the concrete along the straightedge, as shown.

Left:
Run a groover along the control joint cuts you have just made with the trowel. Do not apply too much pressure to the groover or you will leave an impression in the concrete.

Finishing the concrete

When you have completed the edging and grooving of the concrete, you are ready to finish the top surface of the concrete. You have a choice of finishes: smooth, rough, or exposed aggregate.

Smooth concrete. Test the concrete before troweling by running the float over a small surface. If the float brings water to the surface of the concrete, the concrete is not ready for a final troweling. The water at this point can later cause the concrete surface to chip and flake.

For a smooth surface, you must team the float with the steel trowel. First float the concrete surface, then trowel the surface. You will probably have to use a small piece of plywood or hardboard as a kneeboard (shown earlier in this chapter) for this operation.

To operate the float, have the surface of the float flat on the surface of the concrete. Sweep the float in wide arcs, and, at the same time, see-saw it slightly. This will produce a somewhat rough surface. Floating also will help compact the surface of the concrete; it will bring the sand and cement in the concrete mixture to the surface, which is what you want to do.

After you have floated an area, go over the area with a steel trowel. You may trowel concrete several times.

To operate the trowel, press the surface of the trowel flat against the surface of the floated concrete. Move the trowel in wide arcs, just as you did the float. The width of the troweling arcs should be overlapped slightly so that you will not groove the concrete. Hold the trowel at a *very slight angle* so that the edge of the trowel does not dig into the fresh concrete.

When you are finished with this operation, go back and check the edges and control joints you made. If, during floating and troweling, these edges and control joints have been damaged, run the edger or groover again around the forms and across the surface of the concrete.

Rough concrete. A rough surface is easier to create on concrete than a smooth surface. A rough surface can be produced with a wooden float, a metal float, or a broom.

Both the wooden and the metal floats are operated as described in the techniques for smooth concrete. Just omit the troweling procedure and leave the concrete surface to harden after floating it.

For a broom finish, use a wide, fiber-bristled broom such as street sweepers use. This broom has the bristle bulk and weight to make small striations in the concrete. Float the concrete before you finish it with the broom. Start at one edge of the form and pull the broom straight across the concrete to the other edge. Return to the starting edge and repeat the procedure over the entire surface of the concrete, overlapping the sweeps only slightly.

A broom finish is created by dragging a stiff-bristled broom across the fresh concrete. The concrete must be leveled and floated before the broom is used. The broom finish and the float finish, as described in this chapter, are easy to do and require less work than a smooth finish accomplished with a steel trowel.

Exposed aggregate. If you wish an exposed aggregate finish, the surface of the concrete should be about ⅜ inch lower than the top edge of the forms. After the concrete has been leveled, bull float or darby or hand float the surface just as you would for any other finish. Then spread the aggregate over the concrete surface. Make sure the aggregate is distributed over the surface as evenly as possible.

With the bull float, darby, or hand float, embed the aggregate in the concrete with a tamping action. Try to get all the aggregate embedded evenly in the concrete.

When the surface will hold your weight on a kneeboard, take a stiff-bristled broom and brush the surface of the concrete and aggregate lightly. Remove all excess concrete which has been pushed up around the aggregate.

Turn the nozzle of your garden hose to a fine spray. Have a friend spray the surface of the concrete/aggregate as you brush the aggregate with the broom. If, during this process, a lot of aggregate is dislodged from the concrete, stop working until the concrete sets a bit longer. But do not wait too long. As soon as the concrete has set long enough, wash and brush the surface until the water runs off clean and clear and there is no glaze of cement left on the aggregate.

Exposed aggregate finish is accomplished by embedding the aggregate in the concrete, brushing the aggregate, and then, as a final step, washing the surface with water and sweeping the surface with a broom. Here, the redwood forms have been left in the patio for an interesting design. The edges of the concrete within the forms have not been treated with the edging tool.

Curing the concrete

After all finishing work has been done on your concrete patio, the concrete has to "cure." This simply means that the surface of the concrete has to remain damp and warm so that the concrete will harden properly.

There are several ways to cure concrete. The following three methods represent the easiest ways:

- Sprinkle the concrete with a garden hose every morning, noon, and night. If the weather is hot, sprinkle the concrete every three hours during the day for one week.

- Cover the concrete surface with a layer of polyfilm. The polyfilm must be *absolutely* smooth on the concrete surface, and the film must be sealed around the edges of the wooden forms so the film forms an air-tight cover.
- Cover the concrete surface with one layer of burlap. Keep the burlap wet for one week.

After the concrete has cured for one week, gently remove the forms. At this stage the concrete is still "tender" and tends to chip easily when hit around the edges with a hammer or other tools; be very careful when removing the forms.

Building a bull float

The handle of a bull float is a piece of 2 by 2 about 8 feet long. Angle one end of the handle to accept the float. The angle should be about 60 degrees; make the cut with a hand saw. Test the handle on the floor. The handle, with the angle flush on the floor, should be about waist high. If not, recut the angle so that the handle will be comfortable to push and pull on the concrete surface.

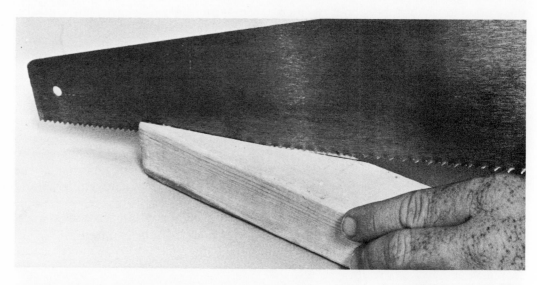

Nail the float to the angle. The float should be a 1 by 6 about 3 feet long; you may cut the float part from a scrap of plywood using the same dimensions. Use 3 or 4 nails to fasten the float to the handle; this joint must be strong.

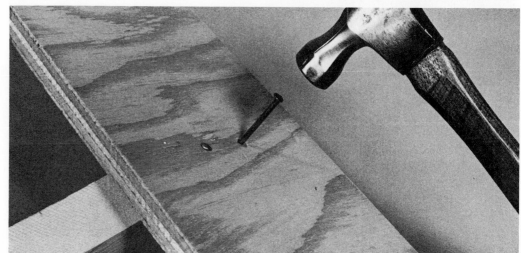

Brace the float with two 1 by 2s angled from the back of the float to either side of the handle, as shown here, fastened with nails. The angle of the braces is not too critical. The bull float is shown in action earlier in this chapter.

Mixing your own concrete

As pointed out earlier, ready-mixed concrete is best for any large patio, driveway, walk, or retaining wall project. However, some handymen may want to mix their own.

Rent a concrete mixer from a rental agency. The mixer may be powered by an electric motor or a gasoline engine. If it is electric, it will probably require a long, extra heavy-duty cord. If the mixer is gasoline driven, you will probably have to have a 5-gallon container of gasoline handy.

You can mix concrete two ways: by volume or by weight. Either way, the objective is to get a proper mixture of Portland cement, sand, fine aggregate, and coarse aggregate. The latter two ingredients may be gravel or crushed stone. To this mixture, you add water. The important ingredients are *cement* (too little makes a weak concrete and too much is a waste) and *water* (too much makes a weak mixture and too little makes a mixture that is hard to spread).

There is a formula that has served civil engineers for generations:

- Enough coarse aggregate to fill the forms—plus 10 percent.
- Enough fine aggregate to fill the voids in the coarse aggregate—plus 10 percent.
- Enough sand to fill the voids in the fine aggregate—plus 10 percent.
- Enough cement to fill the voids in the sand—plus 10 percent.

To this is added the proper amount of water to produce a mixture that will "mound" slightly when it is dumped, instead of slithering out level because it has too much water in it.

You can achieve this mix by buying "con-mix" gravel, and adding cement to it in the proportion of 1 part cement to 4 parts con-mix. On the other hand, if you buy completely raw ingredients, use the following formula:

- 3 parts gravel mix
- 2 parts sand
- 1 part cement

This mixture will appear smooth and solid when you run a trowel across it, even before water is added.

Concrete can also be mixed by weight, as indicated by the first chart in this section. The mixture makes one cubic foot of concrete. You will also find another chart that shows how many cubic feet of concrete are needed for various surface areas and thicknesses of concrete.

CONCRETE COMPONENTS FOR 1 CUBIC FOOT OF CONCRETE (IN POUNDS)

Concrete Materials	Maximum Diameter of Coarse Aggregate	
	¾ Inches	1½ Inches
Cement	25	40
Sand	44	40
Coarse Aggregate	65	75
Water	10	9

CONCRETE IN CUBIC FEET

Concrete Thickness (inches)	Surface Area (square feet)						
	5	10	20	50	100	200	500
2	1.4	2.8	5.5	13.8	27.5	55.0	137.5
4	1.8	3.7	7.3	18.3	36.7	73.3	183.3
5	2.3	4.6	9.2	22.9	45.8	91.7	229.2
6	2.8	5.5	11.0	27.5	55.0	110.0	275.0

If you have access to a commercial scale, weighing is no problem. If you do not have access to one, a bathroom scale is accurate enough unless the weight involved is very small, which is not likely to be the case when you are working with concrete ingredients.

Concrete is always mixed dry, first, before the water is added. This allows the most complete and uniform inter-mixture of sand and cement and aggregates. If you are using a cement mixer, first dump in the coarsest ingredient. Then add the next finest, then the finest, then the cement. Leave the machine running during this procedure for thorough mixing.

When the dry mixing is complete, start adding water—slowly. Watch the mixture in the mixer. It will gradually grow more and more plastic—darker in color—and shinier, as the water mixes in. When the consistency is about like thick mud, and when the mixture is uniform in thickness and in color, let it run for a few minutes more, and it is ready to place.

If you should happen to add a little too much water, remedy the situation by adding a little more cement and sand—about half-and-half—to the mixture, while the mixer is running. If it takes a lot of sand and cement to make the mix the proper thickness, add a little coarse aggregate, too.

When the mixture is perfect, note how much of each component—cement, sand, aggregate, water—went into the mixture; then follow this formula for the rest of the project. The charts here are accurate. However, weather conditions and the amount of water in the sand can throw these formulas off slightly. That is why it is important to run a test batch of concrete before you start the job.

Right:
The moisture content of the sand affects the proportions of the mix when you mix concrete yourself. If the sand is too dry, you must add water; if the sand is too wet, you must reduce the amount of water in the combined mixture of cement, aggregate, and sand. To determine how much moisture is in your sand, ball a handful in your fist and squeeze it. If water runs out of the sand, as shown, the sand is too wet and the mix will need less water.

Far right:
If the sand is too dry, the ball of sand will crumble in your hand, as shown. This means that you must add a slightly larger amount of water to the mixture than the amount specified on the charts in this chapter.

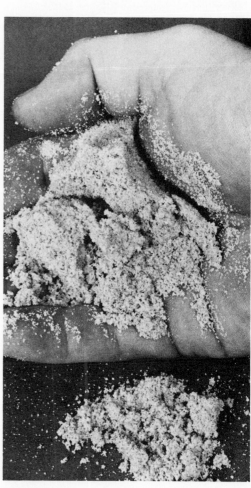

This sand is perfect. It forms a ball in your hand without leaking water or crumbling. As you mix concrete throughout the day, check the sand often for moisture content. Sun and wind tend to dry the sand as the day's job progresses.

Bricks-on-Sand Patios

Placing concrete is a hot and heavy job, and you have to work fast. Laying bricks on a sand base does not take a lot of muscle, and you can take your time. But setting bricks takes a lot of patience, and, unless you have a cushion, the job can be tough on the knees. But aside from these two minor drawbacks, laying bricks on sand is an easy job technically and the result can be most pleasing.

The tools you will need for a brick-on-sand patio project include the following:
  Mason's hammer
  Mason's chisel
  Rubber mallet
  Shovel
  13- or 16-ounce claw hammer
  Garden hose
  Stiff-bristled broom
  Spirit level

All about bricks

There are three grades of bricks available for patio projects: type SW (severe weathering), type MW (medium weathering), and type NW (no weathering). Type MW bricks are recommended for most brick patios; these bricks will hold up under freezing conditions and withstand quite a bit of wear.

All things considered, new bricks are your best bargain as opposed to old or used bricks. Used or old bricks are often crusted with mortar, which must be removed; this is a tedious job. Old bricks most often are soft and will tend to crack and break. However, if you run across a good deal in hard used bricks that do not require a lot of cleaning, buy them.

Standard-size bricks measure 2¼ inches thick, 3¾ inches wide, and 8 inches long. For a 200 square foot patio, you will need 920 bricks, allowing a couple of bricks for breakage. For a 200 square foot patio, you will need 12 cubic yards of sand, if the sand is to be 4 inches thick. From this estimate the materials needed for your patio.

Grading and preparing the forms

The ground on which you lay bricks must be fairly level. If your lot slopes, you might consider a terrace-type patio with several patio levels. In some cases a retaining wall may be necessary. (See the Retaining Walls chapter.)

If your lot is fairly level, you may be able to shovel out the high spots and relocate this dirt in the low spots. If there is a lot of shoveling to do, hire a grading contractor to level the ground for you.

The forms for brick patios are constructed in a manner similar to concrete patio forms. You should have a perimeter form, however, which will be left in position to hold the bricks. If you do not want to leave the form in position, you will have to dig the earth "square" around the perimeter of the project with a flat spade and let the earth serve as a form. The form technique is much easier.

You may also divide the area into halves or quarters with forms just as with a concrete patio, if you plan to leave the forms in position.

Brick patios seldom need to slope for drainage because the joints between the bricks absorb the water. However, if your lot has very hard clay soil, you may want to slope the patio slightly away from the house to make sure that you obtain maximum drainage.

When grading the site, keep in mind that you will have a 4- to 6-inch sand base with another 2½ inches of brick on top of the base; take this thickness into consideration.

Laying the bricks

To construct a brick-on-sand patio, follow these basic steps:
- Grade the site level
- Build the forms
- Place and level a 4- to 6-inch sand base within the forms
- Set and level the bricks
- Fill the joints between the bricks with sand
- Sweep the brick and joint surfaces
- Wet the brick and joint surfaces
- Sweep again
- Water again
- Sweep again

The primary tools in laying brick are a mason's hammer and chisel, shown here. To cut brick to size, form a line at the cut-off point with the chisel end of the hammer. Then, with the chisel, strike the brick along the cut-off line with the hammer. The brick should break cleanly and evenly along this line. It may take a couple of practice bricks before you get the hang of it.

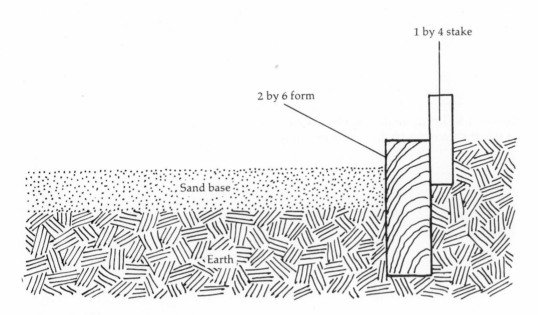

1 by 4 stake

2 by 6 form

Sand base

Earth

A cross-section of the sand base within the forms is shown here. The forms can be 2 by 4s or 2 by 6s, depending on the excavation required. Use 1 by 3 or 1 by 4 stakes to hold the forms in position until the bricks have been set; then remove the stakes. If you plan to remove the forms and replace them with bricks, use ¾-inch thick form boards, but you must allow for the thickness of the bricks—2¼ inches. This requires more digging with a flat spade.

Level the sand base with a screed or strike made with two pieces of board, as shown. A long board (like a screed) spans the width of the forms. The other board is nailed to the longer board to the depth you want the sand to be. Simply run the strike across the sand to smooth and level it. The sand should be fairly damp when you level it. If the sand is too dry, sprinkle it lightly with water from a garden hose.

Brick may be laid in several attractive patterns. The six designs shown here are the most common and the easiest to lay. Notice, however, that the flat herringbone and the running bond patterns require more brick cutting than the other four designs.

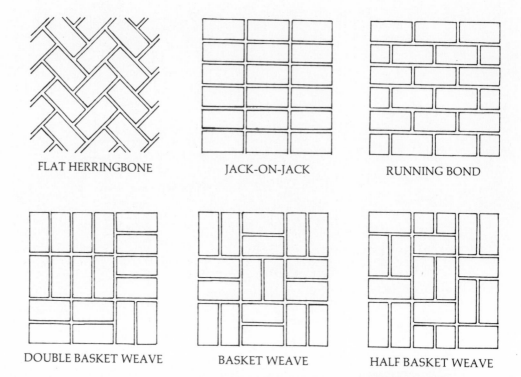

FLAT HERRINGBONE

JACK-ON-JACK

RUNNING BOND

DOUBLE BASKET WEAVE

BASKET WEAVE

HALF BASKET WEAVE

Start laying bricks at one corner of your form and work out into the form. You will have to level the sand as you first get started. When enough bricks have been laid, you can work off the brick surface. Fill each joint with sand as you place the bricks. Tap the bricks level with a rubber mallet, as shown, and check for level often. When the job is complete, sweep sand into the joints until the joints are full. Then wet down the patio with a fine spray from a garden hose. Sweep the area again after the bricks are dry. You will then probably have to add more sand and sweep again. Repeat this process until the joints are tightly packed and will not hold any more sand. If a brick is too low, lift it out and put more sand beneath it.

A cross-section of bricks on sand looks like this. The sand base is 4 inches thick and the joints between the bricks are ½ inch wide. If you do not want to leave the perimeter form boards in position after the patio has been laid, you can remove the forms and insert bricks on edge or on end to fill this void. You do have to make allowances for this, however, when you first form the job; allow room to pry out the forms and to insert the bricks.

Flagstone Patios

A flagstone patio area is not difficult to construct. It is a cross between a concrete patio and a brick-on-sand patio with the element of a jigsaw puzzle thrown in. Flagstones are heavy, and laying them does involve working with concrete. But the job may be done in bits and pieces, so you can head for the hammock when you get tired.

The tools you will need for a flagstone patio project include the following:

13- or 16-ounce claw hammer
Mason's chisel
Sand tamper (which you can make)
Spirit level
Pointed steel trowel
Mortar box for mixing the concrete (use ready-to-mix material)
Hoe to stir the concrete mix
Garden hose
Shovel
Straightedge board for leveling the sand
Spade

Laying the flagstone

The procedure for laying flagstone is similar to laying a concrete or brick patio. The basic procedures are reviewed again below. Turn to the sections on concrete and brick earlier in this chapter for more information.

1. Lay out the job on the ground. The ground must be fairly level, so you may have to excavate the area, cutting down high spots and filling in low spots. It may be necessary to construct a retaining wall. (See Retaining Walls chapter.) In your measurements, allow about 2 inches for the sand base, 1½ inches for the concrete, and 2 inches for the thickness of the flagstone. The thickness of the flagstone may vary; adjust this last measurement with more or less sand.
2. Install the forms around the perimeter of the patio.
3. Place the sand and tamp it until it is firm.
4. Place the concrete in the form sections.
5. Embed the stone in the concrete.
6. Fill the joints with concrete when the base concrete has set.
7. Brush the joints with a broom.
8. Cure the concrete by keeping it wet for several days.

Right:
Lay out the forms and stake them. The forms may be 1 by 6s or 2 by 6s. If the forms are to remain around the patio, trench them into the ground and sink stakes to the ground level to hold the forms in position. Or, you may install the stakes inside the forms and nail the stakes to the forms. In this way, the stone will cover the tops of the stakes. Use redwood or cedar for the forms and stakes.

Far right:
Shovel the sand into the forms. Wet the sand with a fine spray from a garden hose. Level the sand with a screed or strike, and tamp the sand until it is firm. To build your own tamper, use a piece of 4 by 4 post and nail 1 by 3 handles to it, as shown. When the sand has been tamped, sprinkle it again with water. The water—in a fine spray—helps compact and level the sand.

In another part of the yard, lay out the flagstones in the pattern you wish the patio to be. Lay these on the ground with the desired joint spacing—½ to ¾ inches is typical—and work from this area to the formed area. If you have to cut the flagstone, use a mason's chisel, as shown. Flagstone is generally sold by the square yard (about $2 per square yard). And, usually, you have to pick out your own stones at the retail outlet. If your patio will be large, you will have to rent a trailer or truck to haul the stones.

Stir up a mixture of concrete. Dry-mix cement in bags is recommended because you do not have to worry about a large batch of concrete hardening before you can use it. If you mix your own concrete, use 1 part Portland cement to 2 parts sand, mixed with 3 parts finely crushed stone. Mix this formula until it has a medium-thick consistency. Place the concrete over the sand base and level the concrete with a board that has a straight edge. Then lay the stone on top of the concrete. Pick the stones up two or three at a time from the "staging" area, so that all parts of the flagstone puzzle will fit together perfectly. Once the stones are in position, tap them lightly to seat them. Use the handle of the hammer for this.

Fill the joints with the same concrete mixture you used for the base. As you set each stone, level it. You can use a carpenter's level for this; position the level on the top edge of a board that has a straightedge bottom. Since the board will span more area than the level, make the board about 4 feet long. You will need a small trowel to smooth the joints, as shown. When the concrete sets, brush the joints with a broom; this gives a striated effect. Keep the concrete joints wet with water for three days to one week by sprinkling the area lightly with a garden hose. The water makes the concrete "cure" properly.

Wooden Patios

Wooden patios may be built either directly on the ground or over an existing concrete patio. In both methods, construct the wooden patio with 2 by 4s fastened together with 16d nails. The nails should be hot-dipped galvanized, aluminum, or stainless steel nails to avoid rust stains. These stains can ruin the appearance of any wooden structure.

Use at least construction redwood or cedar for the patio; both resist rot and damage by insects. If these woods are unavailable, be sure to purchase wood that has been treated with a wood preservative to prevent decay.

If you plan to build your patio directly on the ground, all vegetation should be removed. You can use a chemical soil sterilant for this, or you can cover the ground with 4-mil polyfilm; the polyfilm will deter the growth of vegetation. Make sure the grade is level so that the framing members sit properly. You will probably have to make final leveling adjustments after the framing is built. If you are placing the patio over a concrete or brick patio, you can level the wooden patio with boards and/or cedar shingles.

A good-sized wooden patio may measure 10 feet by 10 feet, although it can be constructed to almost any size, depending on your design needs. The five 2 by 4 rails in this patio plan are 10 feet long; the 2 by 4 crossrails are toenailed into the rails with 8d nails. A parquet design is achieved by laying the decking at right angles to each adjacent square, as shown in the drawing. Build the foundation grid first, then install the decking. You can precut most of the decking; the perimeter decking should be measured, cut, and fastened piece-by-piece for accuracy.

If your patio design is irregular in shape, lay out the grid foundation over the area you want to cover before fastening the grid together. Although this takes time, you are assured of accurate measurements and will avoid costly mistakes.

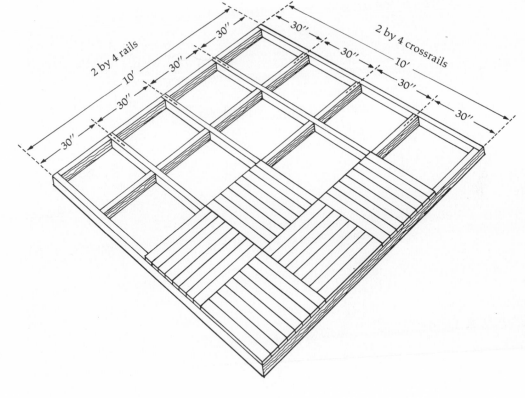

The decking is fastened to the rails in 30-inch lengths. Assemble the rails so that the decking splits the width of a 2 by 4 (3½ inches actual), as shown. At the perimeter of the grid, however, the 30-inch decking extends beyond the center of the 2 by 4 so that it is flush with the outside edges of the 2 by 4 foundation grid. This is shown in the next photograph.

Far left:
Space the decking about ¼ inch apart to allow for drainage. Make a spacer block from ¼-inch thick plywood. Note how the decking extends flush with the foundation grid around the perimeter.

Left:
To avoid splitting the decking, drill pilot holes for the nails along the edges of the decking. Use 16d non-corroding nails to fasten the decking to the rails.

Patio Ideas

Right:
Square clay tiles were used to pave this patio. The tiles are laid on a sand base in the same techniques described for laying bricks on sand. The low brick retaining wall outlines an attractive planting area around favorite trees and shrubs.

Far right:
Simple in design, this exposed aggregate concrete patio offers a secluded living and entertaining area in a garden setting. Decorative concrete block helps define the area; note how the benches in two corners carry out the enclosed feeling without producing a "corral" effect. The wooden forms in the patio were left in position after the concrete was placed and finished.

Permanent forms outlining 4-foot wide strips of exposed aggregate concrete create special interest for this free-form patio. The patio extends into a garden path at the right, giving an extra dimension at little extra cost. Interesting planting areas are created by the shape of this patio, and the design possibilities are endless.

Retaining Walls

Basically, retaining walls act as a dam between two distinct levels of earth; in this capacity they prevent erosion and maintain the grade levels. However, retaining walls may simply offer architectural interest to your patio or deck, or they may be used as planters for flowers and shrubs.

Retaining walls may be constructed with almost any material: concrete, concrete blocks, bricks, railroad ties, logs, stone, corrugated steel roofing, plastic roofing boards, boards, lumber, sewer tile—you name it. Try to match your retaining wall to the patio or other garden structures so that it will blend with the environment. The retaining walls discussed in this chapter, however, are constructed of the more common materials: concrete block, brick, stone, and railroad ties. Other type walls will, for the most part, require construction techniques similar to those discussed; simply adapt the methods to fit your special material or design.

As with any building project, check local building codes before you construct a retaining wall, especially if the retaining wall will affect your neighbor or if it adjoins city property such as a sidewalk or a street. Low retaining walls—next to a patio or those used as a planter—are usually not affected by codes, but you should check before you start construction.

The tools you will need to build a brick or concrete block retaining wall include these:
13- or 16-ounce claw hammer
String
Bricklayer's trowel
Spirit level
Carpenter's square
Mason's chisel
Mason's hammer
Joint strike
Mortar box
Water bucket
Garden hoe
Garden hose

To build a stone retaining wall, the following tools are needed:
String
Spirit level
Mason's chisel
Mason's hammer
Mason's trowel
Shovel
Water bucket

To build a wooden retaining wall, the following tools are needed:
13- or 16-ounce claw hammer
Crosscut saw (or chain saw, if available)
Sledge hammer
String
Spirit level
Broad wood chisel

Concrete Block Retaining Walls

The first step in building a concrete block retaining wall is to dig a trench for the concrete footing. The trench should be dug below the frost line to prevent cracking; check local building codes for specified depths. Once the trench is completed, place the concrete (ready-mixed) for the footing.

The next step is to prepare the mortar. For a wall of standard concrete block construction, the proportions (by volume) for the mortar are 1 part masonry cement to 2 or 3 parts loose mortar sand. Add water, and mix to a whipped cream consistency. If you use Portland cement, mix it 1 to $1^1/_5$ parts hydrated lime and 4 to 6 parts loose mortar sand.

Right:
Set the concrete blocks on a concrete footing, as shown. If corners are involved in the retaining wall, set them first. The corners will serve as a reference point for the remaining courses of block. Use plenty of mortar for the first course of block on the footings.

Far right:
Block courses look like this on the footings. Once you set the base block on the mortar on the footing, do not disturb the block. The blocks should be level and plumb. Check for this frequently.

Trowel the mortar on the blocks as shown. Use plenty of mortar, removing any excess with the trowel. The trick is to keep the mortar continuous throughout the wall. Set about four blocks at one time.

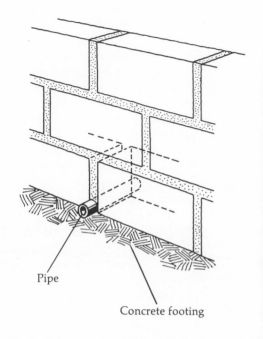

Pipe

Concrete footing

Far left:
Along the base blocks, insert short lengths of ½-inch outside diameter, galvanized steel pipes through the mortar lines. Space these pipes about 4 feet apart. The pipes provide drainage for the earth that the blocks retain.

Left:
Trowel the mortar on the ends of the blocks using a sliding motion with the trowel—as you would butter a cracker. The entire width of the ends should be covered with mortar, as shown, for the best bond.

Far left:
A concrete block wall looks like this as the blocks are laid. The string serves as a leveling guide and is moved with each course of block. You must use a level as you lay the blocks to keep each course level and plumb. Check for level and plumb often; it is very easy to slide the blocks out of alignment, and any small error will compound itself as additional blocks are laid.

Left:
Use a joint strike to smooth the mortar joints in the blocks. Strike the joints as you lay the blocks, and remove any excess mortar with the edge of the trowel. By striking the joints, you make them slightly concave and hard so that they shed water.

Brick Retaining Walls

Brick retaining walls sit on a concrete footing just as do concrete block retaining walls. Construct the footing as you would for block, described earlier in this section. Use SW brick for retaining walls. (See the Materials and the Patios chapters for a discussion of brick types.) As you lay the brick, keep the ready-to-use bricks wet. Either sprinkle these bricks with a garden hose or submerse them in a bucket of water.

If the wall will be fairly high, increase the thickness of the wall at the base and decrease the thickness with the height. This may be done by setting concrete block at the base and facing the block with brick. You should also provide drainage in the wall with ½-inch pipe—as explained for a concrete block wall. The mortar mix is 1 part masonry cement to 3 parts sand. The mortar should be mixed to the consistency of whipped cream. If the mortar is too dry, the bricks cannot be leveled properly. The mortar should ooze out of the joints as the bricks are set. After the bricks have been laid, do not move them. This will destroy the bond. Instead, use plenty of mortar and tap the brick level and plumb.

Mortar should be mixed in small amounts—enough for about 1 hour's work. Otherwise, the mortar will harden before you have the opportunity to use it. When laying a brick wall, start at one end and work across the length of the wall. Do not start at the center.

Lay a bed of mortar on the footing and set the first layer of bricks in position. Trowel mortar on the first course of brick for the next course, as shown.

Tap the bricks level as you set them in the bed of mortar. The mortar joints should be from ¼ inch to ⅜ inch wide. The vertical joints should be from ⅜ inch to ½ inch wide.

Far left:
The ends of the bricks must be covered with mortar. Wipe the mortar on the brick with a sliding motion.

Left:
Remove excess mortar squeezed from the joints by running the edge of the trowel across the face of the brick in a sliding motion. Do this as you lay every two rows of brick.

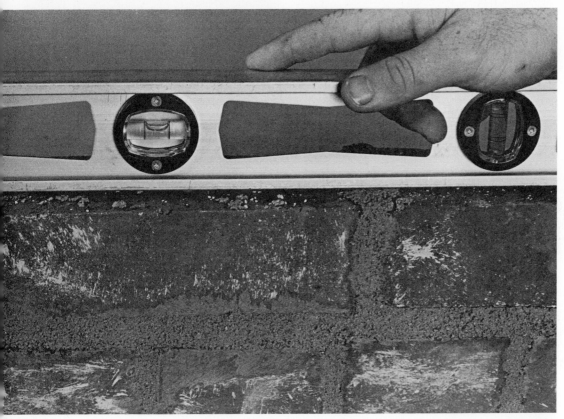

Check the wall for level and plumb as you lay each course of brick. A string stretched along the top course of the bricks will help you keep the wall level. The string must be raised as you proceed with the work (see the section on laying block). As the wall goes up, remove any loose mortar that may stick to the face of the wall with a wire brush. Excess mortar is easier to remove at this point than after it has hardened.

Strike the mortar joints, both the horizontal and the vertical ones, before the mortar has hardened. The strike produces a concave groove in the mortar so that the joint cannot hold water. Striking also improves the appearance of the wall.

Instead of striking the mortar joints, you may leave the joint flush by simply slicing away the excess mortar with a trowel, or you can make a "weathered" joint by sloping the top edge of the mortar with a trowel. The top of the joint is recessed about ¼ inch under the brick course above; the bottom of the joint is flush with the edge of the brick course below. The configuration is a diagonal slant.

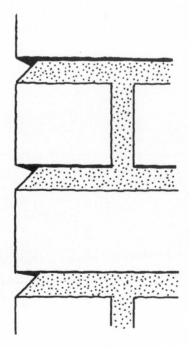

Concrete Retaining Walls

Concrete retaining walls are probably the easiest walls to construct. The only work involved is building the forms from plywood. The forms, however, must be accurately constructed and well braced to withstand the pressure of the concrete once it is placed inside the forms. For the forms, use ¾-inch exterior grade A-D or A-C plywood. The braces should be 2 by 4s. Use ready-mixed cement for this project. (See the Materials and the Patios chapters for a discussion of concrete).

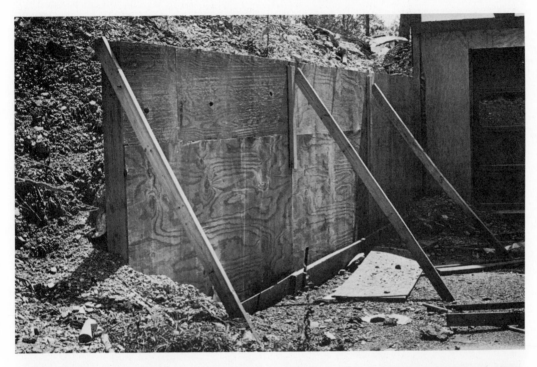

The forms are like a wooden envelope, boxed at each end with a 2 by 6 or a 2 by 8. The wall should extend below the frost line, so you will have to trench the ground and insert the forms in the trench. Reinforce the concrete with reinforcing rods spaced about 2 feet apart. When the concrete is placed (buy ready-mixed material), puddle or spade the concrete into the forms to make sure there are no voids of concrete next to the forms. Place the good side of the plywood (the A face) next to the concrete. Once the forms are full of concrete, smooth the top of the concrete in the forms with a wooden float. Leave the forms in position for at least three days before you strip the forms. Cover the concrete wall with burlap, and keep the burlap wet for at least three days while the concrete cures.

The concrete wall should be smooth after the forms are removed. If there are lines or indentations left by the forms on the face of the wall, smooth these with an abrasive block available at most hardware stores or building materials outlets.

Railroad Tie Retaining Walls

A railroad tie wall is easy to build but you will probably need a helper to help you handle the heavy ties. To cut railroad ties, use a crosscut saw or a chain saw. The chain saw works better, if available.

Railroad ties are treated with an asphalt solution, which tends to build up on the blades of the saws. Remove this gum with mineral spirits. The ties are simply stacked to the height you want the wall to be. (See the Materials chapter for a brief discussion on railroad ties.)

Right:
To anchor the ties in the ground, drill holes through the ties so that the holes match (two holes to each tie). Drive reinforcing rods through the holes into the ground. If the rod is too long after securing the second to the top tie, hammer the rod flat against the tie as shown. The top tie—or the last tie you lay—is not drilled. Instead, toenail this tie to the tie below from the back of the wall with heavy spikes. The top tie hides the rods and the holes.

Far right:
If the railroad tie wall will be low, strengthen the ties by nailing them to stakes driven into the ground, as shown. The stakes should be redwood or cedar or another wood treated with a wood preservative.

This railroad tie retaining wall, shown here at a driveway entrance, is anchored to the earth behind it with reinforcing rods. The rods are bent and hooked into large eyescrews in the ties; the length of the rods are buried in the earth. By staggering the ties atop each other and by creating a stairstep configuration at the ends, it is not necessary to saw the ties to fit exactly.

Stone Retaining Walls

Flat or irregular-shaped stones may be stacked into a wall with or without mortar. The mortar gives the wall more strength; however, you may not need this strength if the wall is a low structure or set on sloping ground. A stone retaining wall usually does not have to be placed on a footing, thereby saving you time and money. The toughest part of building a stone wall is fitting the stones together. For this, you need a mason's hammer and chisel to cut the stones to fit.

Stretch a string along the length of the wall, as shown, to establish the height and to keep the wall as level as possible. The technique is to simply cut the stones to fit and then to stack them on top of each other.

For additional strength, fill the joints between the stones on the backside of the wall with mortar. Use 1 part masonry cement to 3 parts sand. Mix the mortar so that it is somewhat soupy; fling the mortar into the joints with a trowel and use the point of the trowel to pack the mortar into the joints. When the mortar has hardened (wait a week), backfill the wall with dirt.

Right:
A more refined stone wall is laid with mortar between each joint and has a flat flagstone cap to finish off the top. Here, you must chisel the stones to fit snugly, although the mortar will allow for slightly irregular shapes. The same technique is used for this wall as for a loose stone wall. Stretch a string to keep the wall level, and lay each stone in a bed of mortar about ½ to ¾ inch wide. Lay the flagstone cap in a ½-inch bed of mortar; you will have to cut the stone to fit with a masonry chisel.

Far right:
Provide "weep holes" for drainage along the base of the stone wall. You do not have to use pipe for this; a small space is adequate. Space the holes 2 to 3 feet apart. If the wall will be high—5 feet or so—run reinforcing rods between the mortar joints as you build the wall, and bury the rods in the earth behind the wall. Space the rods about 4 feet apart.

A loose stone wall is simply laid on a slope. To build a loose stone wall like the one pictured, work from the bottom of the slope to the top. There may be some cutting necessary; if so, use a masonry chisel or sledge hammer to break the stone. The job is one of fitting the stones together like a jigsaw puzzle.

Index

A

Aggregate, exposed, 70, 84
Aggregates, in concrete composition, 8, 17, 74
Aliphatic resin, 18
Alternating louvered fence, 43, 44
Alternating panel fence, 45
Anchors, masonry. *See* Fasteners

B

Backfill, 93
Barbecue grilles, 30, 36
Basketweave fence, 44
Beams, in deck construction, 21, 23, 26, 28–29
Benches
    in deck construction, 12, 29, 30, 33, 35–38
Bench mark, in deck construction, 23, 25
Boards, 6–7
    sizes (charts), 7, 21
Board and batten fence, 59
Board and board fence, 11, 42
Board batten, 52
Board fence, plain, 60
Board gate, 45
Bolts, 35
Brackets, 33
Bricks, 17, 37
    grades of, 75
    laying, 75–78
    -on-sand patios, 10, 15, 19, 75–79
    patterns, 78
    piers, in fence construction, 59
    retaining walls, 88–90
    setting and leveling, 76–78, 88–89
    size, 75
    types, 75
Bull float, 62, 68, 71
    how to build, 72
Butted corner post joint, 53
Butted top rail joint, 53, 55
Butt joints, 52–55
Butt line post joint, 52

C

Cap board, 52–53
Carpenter's square, 32, 39, 62, 85
Casein, 18
Cedar, 6, 20, 30, 40
Cement, 17, 47, 73
    ready-to-mix, 23
    dry-mix, 17, 40, 74, 81
    mixer, 61–62, 74
Center drop rod, 58
Chain link fencing, 56–58, 59
    line post spacing (chart), 56
    gates, 58
Chemical soil sterilant, 82
Chisels, wood, 39
Clay, 62, 76
Cleated joint, 54
Combination square, 39

Concrete
Concrete. *See also* Aggregates, Cement, Exposed
    Aggregates
    blocks, 23, 84, 86–87
    curing, 71, 79, 91
    dry-mix, 17, 40
    finishing, 70–71
    for fence and gate posts, 46–47, 50, 51, 52, 57
    formula, 57, 73–74, 81
    foundation, 22
    mixing your own, 17, 61–62, 73–74, 81
    patios, 61–84
    piers, in fence construction, 60
    placing, 66–69, 79
    ready-mixed, 17, 61, 66–67, 73, 86, 91
    retaining walls, 91
    rough, 70
    smooth, 70
    tools for, 62
Contractors, 5, 20
Control joints, 69
Costs, estimating, 4
Crossbuck fence, 42
Crushed stone, 8–9, 62
Curves, in patio construction, 62, 65
Cypress, 6, 20, 30, 40

D

Dadoed joint, 52, 54, 55, 60
Darby, 68, 71
Decking, 19–20, 21, 23, 27, 28, 31, 82–83
Decks, 12, 14, 15, 19–38
    building techniques, 19, 23–29
    tools for, 17–18
Diagonal bracing, in deck construction, 29
Dimension lumber. *See* Lumber
Double headers, in deck construction, 31
Drainage
    in fences, 53
    in patio construction, 62, 66, 76, 83
    pitch for, 62, 66
    retaining walls, 88
Drift pin
    in deck construction, 22
    in fence construction, 50, 60
Drop rod, 58

E

Edger, 62, 69
Edging, concrete, 69, 71
Epoxy cement, 65
Exposed aggregate, 70, 84

F

Fascia board, 24, 27, 35
Fasteners, 9–10
    joist hangers, 9
    lag screws, 10, 25, 28–29, 34–35, 52–53
    masonry anchors, 9–10, 25

nails, 17–18, 27, 32, 40–45
    reinforcing rods, 17, 62, 64, 65, 92, 94
    reinforcing wire, 17, 62, 64
    screws, 17–18, 40, 51
    specialty, 18
Fence posts, 41–45, 46–50
Fence rails, 39–45, 49, 50
Fences, 39–60. *See also* particular design
    chain link, 56–58, 59
    materials for building, 39
    on inclines, 49–50
    wooden, 41–45, 49, 50, 52–55, 59, 60
Fence screening, 41, 57, 58
Fence stretcher, 58
Fencing, in deck construction, 30, 32–34
Fiber glass
    in deck construction, 34
    in fence construction, 43
Financing, 4–5
    bank loans, 4–5
    credit unions, 5
    finance companies, 5
    home improvement loans, 5
    open-end mortgages, 5
    reworking existing mortgages, 5
Finishes
    in deck construction, 30
    in fence construction, 40, 41, 42, 44, 45
Finishing, 6
    concrete, 70–71
    in deck construction, 20, 30
Flagstone, in patio construction, 79–81
    laying, 79–81
Flagstone cap, 94
Floating, 70, 71
Floats
    bull, 62, 68, 71, 72
    metal, 70
    wooden, 62, 70
Footings, concrete
    in deck construction, 23, 26
    in retaining wall construction, 86, 88
Fork latch, 58
Forms, 6
    for brick patios, 76–78
    for concrete patios, 62–63, 64, 65, 67, 70–71
        curved, 65
    for concrete retaining walls, 91
    for concrete steps, 65, 66
Foundations
    in deck construction, 20
    in patio construction, 62–64, 82
    in retaining wall construction, 86, 88, 91, 93
Framing. *See also* Forms
    for decks, 19, 20, 34

G

Gate hardware, 40, 51, 58
Gates, 40, 45
    chain link, 58
    latches, 51, 58
    wooden, 45, 51

Glue, 18
Good neighbor fence, 41
Grade work, in patio construction, 62–63, 76
Grapestake fence, 60
Gravel, 8, 17, 62–63
Gravel mix, 46, 73
Grilles, barbecue, 30, 36
Groover, 69
Grooves
    in fence construction, 41
    in patio construction, 69, 70

H

Hardboard, 8, 65, 68, 70
Hardwood, 6
Headers, 30–31
    double, 31

I

Iron railings, in deck construction, 32–34

J

Joining techniques, in fence construction, 52–55
Joints
    in fence construction, 52–55
    in patio construction, 78, 80, 81
Joint strike, 87, 90
Joist hangers, 19, 25, 28
Joists, in deck construction, 19–20, 21, 22, 23–38

L

Lap corner joint, 52
Latex glue. *See* Casein
Ledgers, in deck construction, 19, 23–28, 34–35
Leveling. *See* Grade work
Line post joint, 52
    butted, 52
Line post spacing for chain link fencing (chart), 56
Louvered fence, 44, 60
    alternating, 43, 44
Lumber, dimension, 6–7
    common, 6
    for fences, 40–45
    select, 6
    sizes (charts), 7, 20–21

M

Masonry anchors. *See* Fasteners
Masonry cement, 93
Mason's chisel, 75, 76, 79, 80, 85, 93, 94
Mason's hammer, 75, 76, 85, 93
Measuring
    in deck construction, 19, 20–21, 26
    in fence construction, 48–49
    in patio construction, 63–64, 75, 79
Mitered top rail, 55
Moldings, 8
Mortar, 17, 86, 87, 88, 89, 90, 93, 94
Mortar box, 62, 85
Mortar joints, 87, 88–90

N

Nailing block, 22
Nails. *See* Fasteners

P

Paint, 40, 41, 42, 43
Patios, 9, 10, 14, 15, 19, 61–84
    bricks-on-sand, 10, 15, 19, 75–79
    concrete, 19, 61–74
    design considerations, 9, 10, 15, 61–74, 82, 84
    flagstone, 19, 79–81
    wooden, 82–84
Picket fence, 41
Picket gate, 45
Plumb (level), 23, 26, 48, 50, 89
Plywood, 7–8, 34, 40, 45, 65, 66, 68, 70, 91
    American Plywood Association, 7
    glue bonds, 8
    hardwood-faced, 7
    softwood-faced, 7–8
    veneer grades, 7–8
Polyfilm, 71, 82
Portland cement. *See* Cement
Post anchor, 22, 23
Post and rail fence, 42
Post caps, 11, 33, 43, 45, 52–53
Posthole digger, 39, 46
Posts
    in deck construction, 22, 23–24, 26, 28, 31, 33–38
    in fence construction, 39, 40–45, 46–50, 52–55, 56–57

R

Racking, 49
Rail caps, 38
Rail fences, 42, 49, 52
Railings
    in concrete steps, 66
    in deck construction, 19–20, 30, 32–34, 38
    iron, 32–34
Railroad ties, 8
    in retaining wall construction, 92
Rails, in fence construction, 39–45, 49, 50
Ready-mixed concrete. *See* Concrete
Redwood, 6
    in deck construction, 20, 21, 27, 30
    in fence construction, 11, 40
Redwood and plastic fence, 11, 43
Reinforcing rods, 17, 62, 64, 65, 92, 94
Reinforcing wire mesh, 17, 62, 64
Retaining walls, 62, 76, 85–94
    brick, 84, 88–90
    concrete, 91
    concrete block, 86–87
    railroad tie, 92
    stone, 93–94
Riser forms, 66

S

Sand, 8
    in concrete composition, 8, 17, 73–75
    in patio construction, 62, 70, 73–74, 75, 76–77, 78, 80
    moisture content, 74–75

Saws, 32, 34, 39, 41, 54, 62, 85
Screeding, 63, 67, 77, 80
Screening
    in deck construction, 12, 34, 38
    in fence construction, 39, 43, 44, 52, 55, 58
Screws. *See* Fasteners
Seats, in deck construction, 29, 30, 33, 35–38
Shear (downward pressure), 53, 54
Shovel, square-nosed, 62
Slag, 62
Slate, 17
Slopes, 38
    building fences on, 49–50
    for drainage, 76
Softwood, 6, 20
Spacer blocks, 27
Spading, in patio construction, 67
Spring catch, 58
Spring latch, 58
Stains, 30, 40. *See also* Finishes
Steps
    concrete, 65, 66
    in deck construction, 20, 32, 36–38
    in patio construction, 65
Stone
    artificial, 17
    crushed, 8, 17, 62
    dressed, 17
    retaining walls, 93–94
    semidressed, 17
    undressed, 17
Straightedge, 69, 81
Stretcher bar for chain link fences, 58
Striking, in patio construction, 67, 68, 80

T

Tamper, 79
    how to build, 80
Template, 41
Tension bands, for chain link fences, 58
Tension bar, for chain link fences, 58
Tiles, in patio construction, 84
T latch, 51
Toenailed joint, in fence construction, 54
Top rail joint, butted, 53, 55
Top rail, mitered, 55
Treads, stairstep, 32, 66
Trees, in deck construction, 15, 30–31, 38
Trowels, 69, 70, 81, 86, 87, 88, 93
    bricklayer's, 85
    pointed, 69, 79
    steel finishing, 62, 70

V

Veneer grades (plywood), 7–8

W

Walls, retaining. *See* Retaining walls
Weepholes, 94
Wire cutters, 39
Wire, reinforcing mesh, 17, 62, 64
Wood preservative, 40
Wood finishes, 30, 40–45
    paint, 40, 41, 42, 44, 45
Wrought iron. *See* Iron railings